The Quilter's Guide *to* Rotary Cutting

SECOND EDITION

DONNA POSTER

krause publications

700 East State Street, Iola, WI 54990-0001
www.krause.com

Please call or write for our free catalog of publications. Our toll-free number to place an order or obtain a free catalog is 800-258-0929 or please use our regular business telephone 715-445-2214 for editorial comment and further information.

Black and white photography by Cindy Vaughn
Color photography by Kris Kandler
Book design by Jan Wojtech
Manufactured in the United States of America

Library of Congress Cataloging-In-Publication Data

Poster, Donna
    The quilter's guide to rotary cutting, 2nd edition
    1. title   2. quilting   3. rotary cutting

ISBN 0-87341-707-0
CIP 98-87369

ACKNOWLEDGMENTS

Special thanks to the following persons and companies:

Hobbs Bonded Fibers, Waco, TX, for the Heirloom Cotton batting used in all of the quilts made by Donna Poster

Holiday Designs, Mineola, TX, for the rotary-cutting templates used in Donna's Speedy Cutting System.

The delightful ladies who stitched models for this second edition. A very special thank you to Linda Crabtree, Sarah Francis, Susan Gradick, Barbara Johnson, JoAnn Long, Brenda Place, Josephine Rainwater, Dotti Reynolds, Janet Warner, and Connie Tzu-Hsun Wu for their help and their friendship.

Cindy Vaughn for the photographs of all the quilters having a good time stitching in my studio, Donna's Place.

Debbie Luttrell for the fun we all have in her quilt shop, Stitchin' Heaven in Quitman, TX.

Kay Costner and Susan Stallings of The Quilting Loft for their care and creative stitching in the models they machine-quilted.

Amy Tincher-Durik for the loving care she gave this book.

Robbie Fanning for being my mentor in the world of publishing and for becoming my friend in life.

Zoë and Laura Pasternack for their encouragement and never-ending faith in me.

Arn Poster, who, besides developing the templates that made all this possible, once again cooked great meals, walked the dogs, and put up with the endless bellyaching that is part of writing my books.

DEDICATION

Parents can give their children two things.
The one is roots and the other is wings.
With loving thanks to
My father, L.Harry Kershner, for giving me roots
And my mother, Alma Sitler Kershner, for giving me wings

CONTENTS

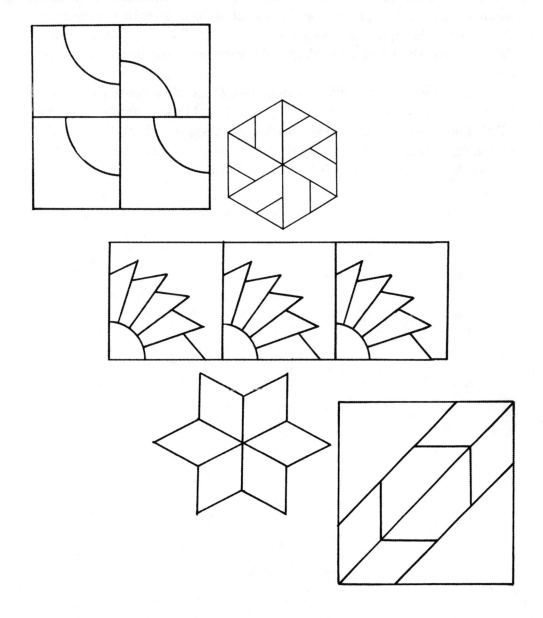

FOREWORD

Even though the rotary cutter has revolutionized sewing and quilting, I know an intelligent grown-up who has sewn for years and who is still afraid of using her cutter. She's undoubtedly the tip of the iceberg.

Enter Donna Poster, queen of the speed-cut quilt. Donna's first book, *Speed-Cut Quilts*, showed how to use a rotary cutter and plastic templates to speed-cut 1,200 quilt blocks. Best of all, she organized us with a step-by-step Play-Plan: no more bare beds because of inertia. In that first book, she used her tools to cut specific blocks, like making Christmas cookies with bell-, tree-, and wreath-shaped cutters.

But Donna has a what-if mind. What if I did this and this and this with the templates and the cutter? Couldn't I cut any shape?

The results are this new, revised book, a broader guide than her first. Now you can make any shape of cookie cutter. The key is to determine the needed width, cut lots of strips, then chop shapes out of them. To help you practice, Donna has included instructions and templates for 20 quilts. With her usual thoroughness, she's figured yardages for seven sizes and offered alternate designs.

My friend with rotary cutter phobia, however, needs a house call. Since Donna runs a quilt shop, teaches, and travels, I doubt she'll stop by. But you could. Look outside your circle of fearless sewers and quilters. Does someone on the iceberg need help? Why not take your rotary cutter, template, mat, and this book to that someone's home for a few hours?

Robbie Fanning

PREFACE

Hundreds of years ago, women made quilts by spinning the yarn and weaving the fabric. Only then could they begin to cut and sew.

Future generations bought their fabric at the store and their grandmothers said, "Hmph! In my day we made our own fabric."

Then came the sewing machine. Those of our grandmothers who were fortunate enough to own one proudly used it to stitch their quilts. Their grandmothers said, "Hmph! In my day we pieced our quilts by hand."

Now we have the rotary cutter, and we're whipping out quilts like mad. And our grandmothers are saying, "Hmph! In my day we cut out each piece with scissors."

Following this progression, I have a vision of one hundred years from now. Florabene is going to make

a quilt. She hires a babysitter for little Cassiopeia (some things never change) and heads for the local quilt shop. There she selects her fabric and rents an hour on the quilting machine. This piece of equipment is about the size of a small room with hundreds of dials, buttons, and slots on the front. Florabene selects her quilt pattern, colors, and dimensions, then carefully feeds her fabric into the chosen slots. With all systems ready, she now pushes a central button that activates the machine. Buttons light up, dials turn, things go buzz, whiz, and cachunk, cachunk!

Forty-five minutes later, with one huge belch, this machine spits out a gorgeous, finished quilt.

And our children, now grown up and grandmothers themselves, will undoubtedly say, "Hmph! In my day, we speed-cut our quilts with rotary cutters…"

INTRODUCTION

As a quiltmaker, teacher, and shop owner I have been fascinated by the rotary cutter ever since the day I sliced up my first pile of fabric. It seemed to me, however, that we should be able to do more with such a wonderful tool than cut strips and triangles.

After much experimentation, I finally developed a series of plastic diamond and hexagon templates and my husband, Arn, began Holiday Designs to produce them. As an engineer, however, he was hardly willing to stop there. He began developing a vast range of cutting templates, including several he was told couldn't be done.

I began using these templates in my sampler classes with much success and soon compiled these methods into my first book, *Speed-Cut Quilts.*

At this point I was running a quilt shop, teaching classes, and writing a book, which left me little time for stitching. So every time I got antsy and simply had to go to the sewing machine, I'd look over these templates to see if there was anything I could use to get them cut out fast. I was amazed at how much I could do with them.

Eventually, I came to realize that almost every piece in every pieced quilt could be speed-cut. I was ecstatic.

For more than a year I experimented on quilts, fabric, and with students to bring you *The Quilter's Guide to Rotary Cutting*, 1st Edition. With it you could take almost any quilt book you already own, plus any you may buy in the future, and translate the quilts to speed cutting.

The book became a huge success, but I soon realized I should have included more information and quilts for the beginner. So I was delighted when I was offered the chance to do a second edition and add these things.

To make this revised edition more interesting I have included instructions for 20 quilts, including four new ones, using my speed-cutting methods. Each quilt has all of the yardages and cutting information for seven sizes, including a tablecloth/lap-throw (the square or oblong size). I have also included several options with each, plus a drawing that includes the seven sizes so it can be copied and cut to the size being made. In this way you can view the full quilt and actually count the number of pieces needed. Copy the page several times and have great fun filling it in with a #2 pencil or a box of colored pencils.

Some of the quilts are familiar old favorites, some are hard-to-find patterns of old favorites, and some are brand new. I've tried, whenever possible, to be authentic in naming these quilts, but many of the patterns came to me in the same way that quilt patterns, over the years, have always been passed around. So you may know some of these by a different name.

I have included a section on basic construction techniques. These are the ones I've found, in my classes, to work best for the most people. I feel strongly, however, that quilters must read, listen, experiment, and learn as many hints, techniques, and variations as possible. Gather up a never-ending fund of knowledge, then choose whatever works best for you. Students in my beginner classes all hear my "ten quilters" story. I tell them that if there are ten quilters in the same room, all doing the same thing, they are doing it ten different ways. And they are all correct!

So here's my newest book, I've had a wonderful time writing it—I hope you have a wonderful time using it!

Donna

1 MAKING YOUR FIRST QUILT: BEGINNER'S PRACTICE

If you're making your first quilt, please browse through this entire book to become familiar with it—but don't expect to understand much of it. This book is meant to lead you from the very beginning stages of quilting all the way through to advanced stages. Let's do this gently.

First, you'll need to do some basic practicing. Oh, hush now—I know you want to jump right in and start that quilt in the Advanced section. Please don't. You'll hate it and probably never make another quilt. With a few practice sessions followed by an easy quilt, you'll form good habits that will make all of your quilting a real pleasure for the rest of your life! Here's what you'll need:

1. Good quality, 100% cotton fabric (muslin is just fine to practice on)

2. Rotary cutting equipment (see my recommended Starter Set, pages 10-13)

3. Sewing machine, thread, and favorite sewing tools

Got all that? OK, let's practice:

Step 1. Practice cutting. See Chapter 3, Basic Techniques of Rotary Cutting. Practice all of the steps including making a triangle (pages 14-17). (Actually **do** all of this; it's much better than just reading about it.) Cut three 2˝ wide strips for the next step.

Step 2. Practice sewing. See The 1/4˝ Seam (pages 30-31). Sew the three strips together.

Step 3. Practice pressing. See Pressing (page 34). Press the two seams.

Step 4. Measure the width of this set of strips. If it measures 5˝, your seam allowances are perfect! If it's wider than 5˝, you'll need to widen your seams a bit. If it's narrower than 5˝, your seams are a bit too wide. Practice this until you can maintain a perfect seam allowance.

The three techniques you just practiced are the key to good quilting. Don't try for perfection right away, but try to remember, as you're learning, that these will make your quilting much easier: (1) **careful cutting**, (2) **attention to seam allowances**, (3) **"easy-does-it" pressing**.

Now you're ready for more fun! Try:

(1) Using the Basic Strips (page 17)

(2) Donna's Speedy System (pages 20-22). Use the template A from Piney Woods for this practice piece.

Now let's make a quilt! The very easiest is the Nine-Patch Chain. Start with a small one; maybe a crib or lap (oblong) size. Have fun and don't keep ripping out every little imperfection. This is a "learning" piece and will not be hung in the Smithsonian! If you enjoy making this quilt, you'll make another, then another, and that's the way you'll become a really great quilter.

THE BASIC CONSTRUCTION PROCESS

Step 1. Preparation
    Choose the design, size, and colors for your quilt
    Purchase the fabric and the batting
    Gather all of the supplies and equipment needed

Step 2. Cutting
    Preshrink the fabric
    Make or tape all of the cutting templates
    Cut all of the pieces for the quilt top

Step 3. Sewing
    Piece the quilt top
    Add the borders

Step 4. Finishing
    Mark the quilting lines
    Baste and quilt the layers together
    Finish the outside edges

Step 5. Enjoy your quilt!

2 SPEED-CUTTING EQUIPMENT

The recent development in tools has given today's quilters many more delightful options than their grandmothers had. No longer do we have to spend days drawing and cutting around each separate piece for a quilt.

The secret to this new method of cutting is to get good equipment and learn to use it effectively. With the rotary cutter and my Speedy System you can turn almost any pieced quilt pattern into a speed-cut project.

The time you'll save will astonish you. The first time I needed 792 odd-shaped pieces for a queen size quilt top, I timed myself. It took 1 hour and 15 minutes, and the pieces were so accurate that the sewing was a breeze.

The system I've developed involves the use of generic templates, taped, to define the pattern piece being cut.

There are dozens of templates currently on the market which are used for specific quilts. I have included several of these in the book, plus alternative uses for them. For example, the template for the Love Ring makes a fine corner piece for the Fan.

You'll find many advantages to my system. For the first time, hand-piecers can enjoy the speedy methods, too. Instead of cutting across seams on pieced strips, you quickly cut stacks of pieces which can easily be hand-pieced.

Specialized fabrics that would be difficult to draw shapes on, such as lamé, are a cinch to cut with the rotary cutter.

Specific placement of fabric designs is easy with the see-through acrylic templates.

Mirror-image patterns are cut by simply flipping the template over or by stacking all of layers with like sides together.

The accuracy in cutting is nothing short of a stitcher's dream. Imagine cutting 12 layers of fabric even with the finest of scissors. It would be almost impossible to cut the top and bottom layers the same. With the rotary cutter, they are identical. Cut edges are straight, even, and precise, making the stitching a snap.

These time-saving tools make piecing much easier and enjoyable. Our goal, of course, is to have a lovely quilt when finished, but how much nicer it is when we've also enjoyed the process of making it.

CHOOSING YOUR EQUIPMENT

Anyone who has shopped for cereal lately knows the confusion of choosing one brand. The world of the rotary cutter is no less confusing to the novice.

As with all equipment, there are pros and cons for all of the types available. What appeals to Sally may be objectionable to Nancy.

I hope the following comments will help you decide which equipment to purchase. They are based on observations made by my students over the many years I've been teaching classes on using the rotary cutter.

In this chapter, I will discuss basic equipment (i.e., rotary cutter, cutting mat, and rotary cutting rulers and templates), helpful extras, and my recommended starter set. Other quilting equipment is described in Chapter 4.

BASIC EQUIPMENT

Rotary Cutter

This is a cutting tool, resembling a pizza cutter, with a very sharp, circular blade. Because the blade is so sharp, a guard is necessary.

All of the cutters currently available seem to be of good quality and are sturdy and easily adapted to right- or left-hand use. They all include high-quality blades. Replacement blades are readily available.

Some cutters are available in two or three different sizes. For straight edges, the larger, heavy-duty cutters are easier to use, cut faster, and give you better control. Curves can be cut more easily with the smallest size.

The following brands all lock in place when open and are simple to close. My students and I have noticed these differences:

Olfa: Features a guard that is easily clicked on. I teach my students to "push that thumb" at the end of **every** cut. After a short time, this becomes an automatic movement.

Fiskar's, Dritz, and Quilter's Rule: The shaped handle on any of these three brands is easy to grasp and appeals to many people with arthritic or handicapped hands. They can also be held quite comfortably when cutting through multiple layers of fabric.

Cutting Mat

I strongly recommend that you invest in a self-healing mat specifically made for use with the rotary cutter. Using any other type of surface will quickly dull the blade, and having to constantly replace the blade is costly and aggravating.

In purchasing a mat, look for these points:

1. **Size**. One edge of any mat should be at least 23-24″ long to accommodate a folded piece of 45″ wide fabric. The standard 18″ x 24″ is great for toting to classes. For home use, treat yourself to the biggest one you can afford or have room to store. (A friend of mine stores hers under the bed.)

2. **Finish**. A matte finish with a slightly rough feel will help keep your fabric from slipping. The slicker the surface, the more difficult it is to use.

3. **Grids**. Many mats are available with 1″ grids on one side—nice but not necessary. My students learn all techniques without using the grid lines.

Most mats must be stored flat and away from extreme heat. If not, they will warp. Several mats are light on one side and dark on the other. This feature is most helpful to people who have difficulty distinguishing color or tones.

Rotary Cutting Ruler and Templates

Here's where you enter the world of mass confusion. With dozens of rulers and templates on the market, how does a beginner pick and choose?

First, understand the difference between specialized templates and general-use templates. Specialized templates are used for only one shape. To make all of the quilts you dream of, using only specialized templates would mean buying hundreds.

Instead, with my Speedy System, you can use a

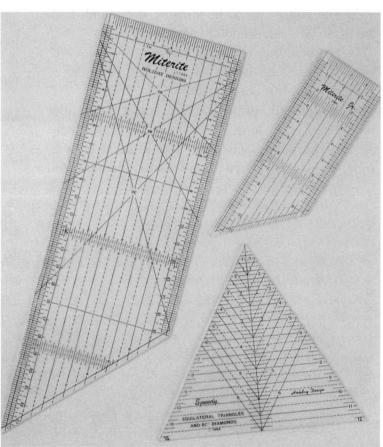

The Miterite ruler, Miterite Jr., and the Equilateral Triangle/60° Diamond Template, all from Holiday Designs.

general-use template for many shapes. You merely tape different areas on the general-use template for cutting guidelines. For example, with my Speedy System, you can cut a hexagon with a 60° diamond template.

Even though I will give you many options for templates, many specialized templates simply cannot be substituted. In Appendix B, I have included instructions for using only two of these for a second purpose. Learn to look at all specialized templates with an eye to other uses.

I've set up some guidelines for you to follow, but you will eventually have your own favorite assortment of templates. Purchase them with an eye to variety and ease of use.

Rulers and templates to be used with the rotary cutter are very different from those meant for other uses. You'll need to look for these points:

1. They should be made of sturdy, clear acrylic and be a bit over 1/16″ in thickness (so that the blade will not cut them).

2. The edges should be straight, not rounded, so the blade will ride smoothly against them.

3. The markings should be easy to read, with 1/8″ and 1/4″ markings easily distinguished from the 1″ markings and from each other.

4. The length of your basic strip-cutting ruler should be 23-24″, long enough to span a folded piece of 45″ wide fabric. The ruler should be at least 6″ wide, because narrow rulers are more difficult to hold

in place. My personal favorite is my husband's Miterite, which is 8″ wide and cut at a 45° angle on one end, because it serves a wide variety of purposes.

5. The surfaces should be smooth enough so that they slide easily. This helps in accurately positioning the rulers and templates on the fabric.

HELPFUL EXTRAS

1/4″ Quilter's Tape

The best tape to use on your templates. It is narrow and leaves little residue. Whenever possible, apply it to the **unprinted** side of your template. If you must use it on the printed side, use very small amounts and remove it as soon as possible.

WD40 or Goo Gone

Excellent products for removing any tape residue.

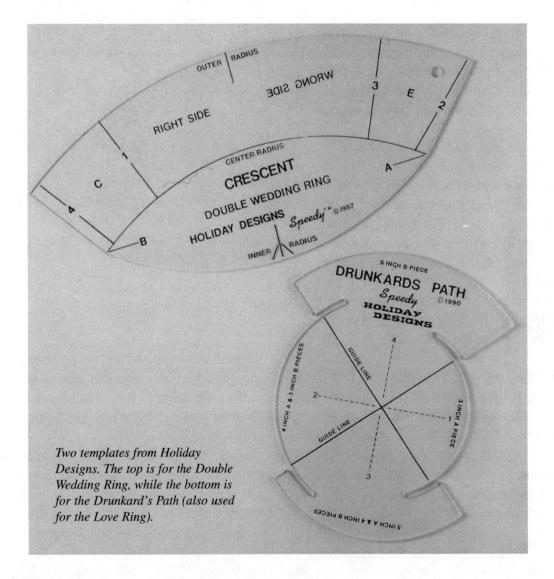

Two templates from Holiday Designs. The top is for the Double Wedding Ring, while the bottom is for the Drunkard's Path (also used for the Love Ring).

Rotary Cutter Replacement Blades

Always keep extra blades handy because they will get dull or nicked in time. Whenever I'm about to cut out a whole quilt—12 layers at a time—I change blades. It's worth it for the time it saves and the resulting neatness. A hint on changing blades: As you remove the cutter parts, lay them down in the order you took them off. When you get to the blade, change it, and the parts are all lined up, ready to put back in the correct order.

Safety Note: I put the old blade in the packaging from the new blade, then tape it heavily before discarding it.

Slide and Grip Strips

These grip the fabric when you press down on the template, keeping it firmly in place. Use small pieces, about 1/2″ square, sparingly, because you'll want to slide the template when positioning it. I place them 1/4″ in from all cutting edges, about 4-6″ apart. Put them on the top and bottom, so you can turn the template over if needed.

Handle

A handle may be attached to the top side of the template, making it much easier to reposition for the next cut without mussing your pile of fabric. Also, the lines on your template will last much longer because you'll be lifting it rather than sliding it, which will eventually erase some of the lines. These handles are easily removed as needed.

AND EVEN MORE

In the last few years, an incredible number of rotary cutting notions, products, and gizmos have arrived in the marketplace. You'll see them in your favorite shops, catalogs, and magazines. Packages of templates which combine to make many quilts, wide rulers with slots for cutting many strips without ever moving the ruler, blade sharpeners…the list goes on! Will you like what you buy? Some, yes; some, no. If you're hesitant about a product, try to find someone who has used one. (If you are on the Internet, you'll find plenty of opinions!) If all of this fails, go ahead and try it. That one lifesaver you discover is worth all of the others that end up, unused, in a drawer.

MY RECOMMENDED STARTER SET

Medium-size Cutter (1-3/4″ blade)
18″ x 24″ Mat
Spare Blade
Ruler. For squaring corners and cutting strips, bias tape, 45°, 90°, 135° triangles, angles, and mitered borders. I prefer my husband's Miterite by Holiday Designs.
12-1/2″ Square. For squaring corners and blocks, cutting squares, and rectangles from 1/2″ to 12-1/2″.
60° Diamond. For cutting 30°, 60°, and 120° triangles and angles.
1/4″ Quilter's Tape

These pieces would set up a very basic rotary-cutting system. Add pieces as you need them.

All of the supplies mentioned in this chapter are available in quilt shops. If you do not have access to a quilt shop, you can order them by mail from the Supply List at the end of this book.

3 BASIC TECHNIQUES OF ROTARY CUTTING

Using the edge of a ruler or template as a guide, just roll the cutter blade through layers of fabric to cut it.

Yes, it really is as simple as that! But there are ways to make cutting even easier. Here's how:

Handling the Fabric. Fold the fabric as it was folded on the bolt, keeping the selvages even. If the layers do not lie smoothly, do not force them. Just lift the top layer and move it gently to one side until it automatically lies flat. Position fabric on the cutting mat (Fig. 3-1). (A left-handed person will lay the fabric on the left side of the mat.) To cut multiple layers, stack them with the folds even and the selvages parallel. I cut as many as 12 layers. Practice first!

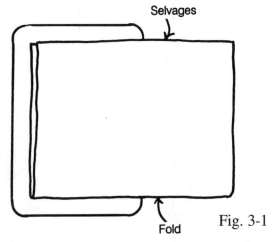

Selvages

Fold

Fig. 3-1

Handling the Ruler. Holding your left hand like a tent, place your thumb and forefinger 1/2″ to 1″ in from the cutting edge with remaining fingers in a comfortable position (Fig. 3-2). Press down firmly. This prevents the ruler from moving and presses the layers of fabric firmly together. When cutting a 22″ span, press on the one end of the ruler while cutting, then, carefully walking your hand to the other end, finish cutting.

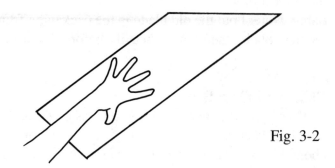

Fig. 3-2

Handling the Cutter. Pull the guard back to expose the blade. Hold the cutter at a comfortable angle, with the blade side next to the ruler (Fig. 3-3). The blade must be perpendicular to the ruler. If held at an angle away from the ruler, it will damage both the ruler and the blade (Fig. 3-4). As you cut, press the cutter down firmly and slightly against the ruler. Always cut away from you because this gives you the best control. Be sure to flick the guard on at the end of **every** cut. Safety measures are extremely important. Treat the cutter with the same measures of caution that you use with kitchen knives and sewing shears.

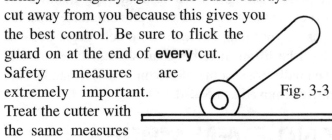

Fig. 3-3

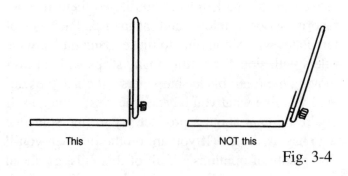

This   NOT this

Fig. 3-4

USING THE RULER

The portion of the ruler on the fabric will determine the size of the piece you'll cut. For example, when cutting a 2″ strip, place 2″ of the ruler on the fabric and let the rest hang off (Fig. 3-5).

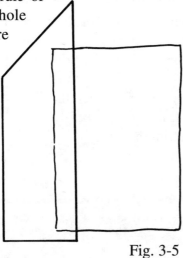

That's my general rule of thumb for my whole Speedy System. Here are some other rules to follow:

The first cut on any piece is made to trim the raw edge of the fabric. This cut must be 90° to the fold. Otherwise, instead of the strips being straight, they will be angled (Fig. 3-6).

Fig. 3-5

There are several ways to do this. My favorite is to place the 1″ crossmark of the ruler on the fold. The cutting edge is then at a 90° angle (Fig. 3-7). You'll need to move to the other side of the table to make this cut (**never** try to cut under your arm!).

A second method is to place a large square template on the fold to determine the 90° angle, then position the ruler against it (Fig. 3-8). Carefully remove the square and cut against the ruler. Caution: It is easy to move the ruler out of position without realizing it.

A third method can be done only on a gridded mat. Place the fold on one of the horizontal lines and line up the ruler with a vertical line (Fig. 3-9). This is a fast and easy method, but you must be careful to keep the fold on that line. If your mat has a slick surface, use this method.

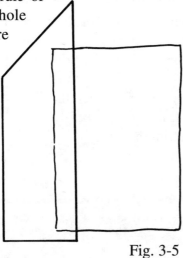

Fig. 3-6

Fold

Always position the ruler 1/2″ or more below the starting point of a cut. Otherwise, you'll nick the corner of the ruler and very quickly ruin the blade (Fig. 3-10).

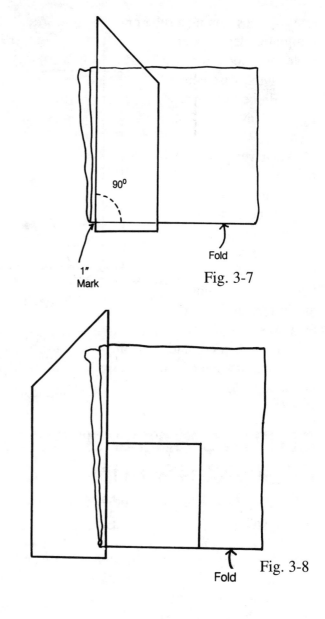

90°

1″
Mark

Fold

Fig. 3-7

Fold

Fig. 3-8

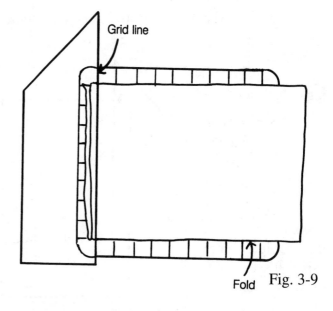

Grid line

Fold   Fig. 3-9

When positioning a ruler or template, lean over the table and look straight down. Otherwise your cut will be wrong by the thickness of the ruler.

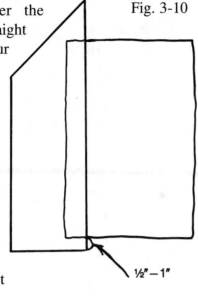

Fig. 3-10

½″ – 1″

Whenever possible, use the same ruler throughout a project, because all rulers are not exactly alike. With my Speedy System, however, this is not as important as it once was.

Note: I've tried cutting batting—it doesn't work! The blade just imbeds all of those little white fibers into a never-to-be-healed slice in the mat.

CUTTING BASIC STRIPS: BEGINNER'S FUN

Let's have some fun now! You've learned the basic cutting techniques, and it's time to try a few strips. Practice first! If you don't have any scraps of good quality fabric (poor fabric will behave badly and dull your blade), invest in a yard or two of good muslin. The practice time will be well worth it.

Step 1. Trim fabric (Fig. 3-7).

Step 2. Place the 3″ ruler marking on the trimmed edge (Fig. 3-11).

Step 3. Cut!

You've done it! No fooling—that's all there is to cutting strips.

Now here are a few hints for cutting lots of strips:

Put some 1/4″ masking tape on the ruler line you're using. It's too easy to whiz along, be distracted, and

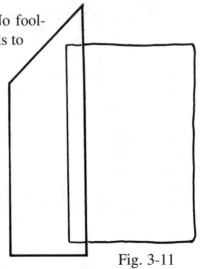

Fig. 3-11

plunk that ruler on the wrong line. The tape will catch your attention. Note: Always put the tape **outside** the cutting line. The tape should never end up on the piece to be cut (Fig. 3-12). Tape on the unprinted side of the ruler whenever possible so you don't pull off the printing.

After every third or fourth strip, check the 90° angle. If it's off a bit, retrim the edge.

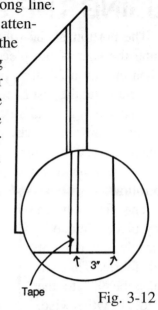

Tape

3″

Fig. 3-12

Connie (l.) and Susan sharing hints on rotary cutting.

MORE BEGINNER'S FUN

Just for fun, let's cut some squares from that strip you just made.

Step 1. Trim end of strip to 90° (Fig. 3-13).

Step 2. Place the 3″ ruler line on the trimmed edge (Fig. 3-14).

Step 3. Cut.

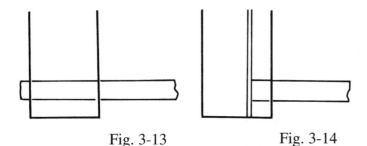

Fig. 3-13   Fig. 3-14

Now is this fun or what? Do a few more. Just keep aligning the cut end of the fabric with the 3″ line of the ruler and cut (Fig. 3-15).

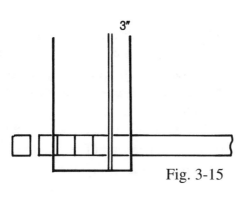

Fig. 3-15

Want a rectangle? Move the cut end to the 5″ ruler line (and move the tape) and cut (Fig. 3-16).

How about some triangles? Just place the ruler from corner to corner on one of the squares (Fig. 3-17). Cut.

It's so easy! All you do is cut some strips, then chop your pieces out of that strip.

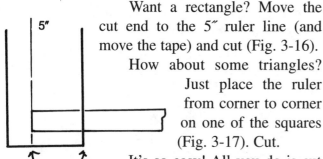

Fig. 3-16

You've just opened the door to a whole new world. Now come along with me and I'll show you, one by one, how almost every quilt piece in any quilt can be cut like this!

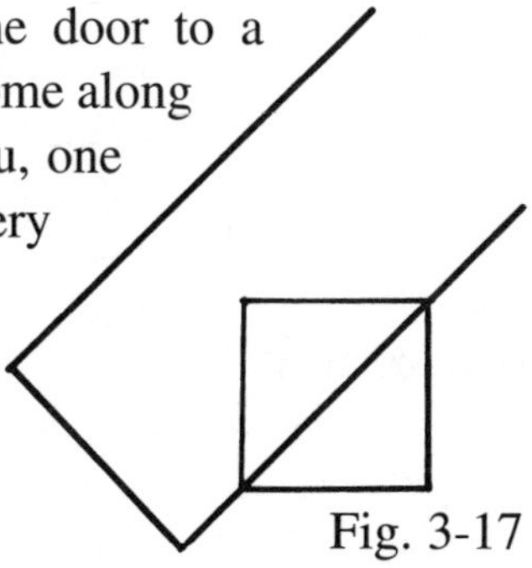

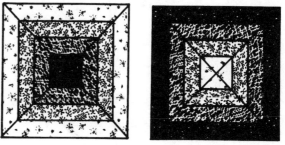

Fig. 3-17

USING THE BASIC STRIPS

Cutting strips is the basis of almost all rotary cutting. Following are some of the most common uses of these strips. Play with these a bit—they're fun. (Cut 2″ strips throughout.)

Cutting Across Multiple Strips to Form Units

1. Sew two strips. Cut units same width (2″ here) as original strips (Fig. 3-18).

2. Turn alternate units 180°. Stitch together (Fig. 3-19).

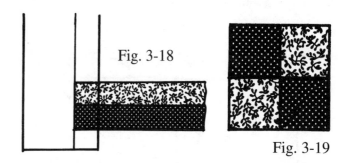

Fig. 3-18

Fig. 3-19

Cutting Shapes From Units of Strips

1. Sew several strips. Cut triangles (Fig. 3-20).

2. Turn units. Stitch together (Fig. 3-21).

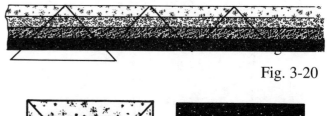

Fig. 3-20

Fig. 3-21

Cutting Bias Strips

With the rotary cutter this method is faster than any other I've found.

1. Trim end of fabric so it forms an exact 90° angle (Fig. 3-7).

2. Open to single thickness. Fold cut edge to meet selvage edge (Fig. 3-22).

3. If length of diagonal fold is longer than ruler, fold upper point down to the lower point (Fig. 3-23).

4. Remove diagonal folded edge by trimming 1/8″ from it (Fig. 3-24).

5. Cut bias strips of desired width (Fig. 3-25).

6. Sew bias strips end to end, right sides together, with a 1/4″ seam (Fig. 3-26).

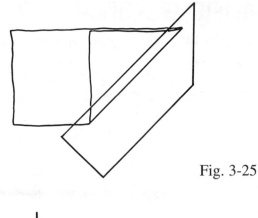

Fig. 3-25

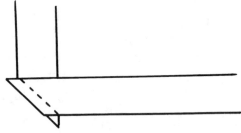

Fig. 3-26

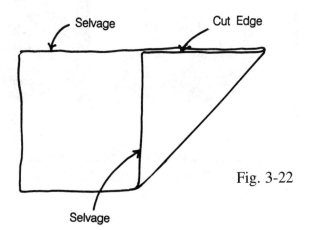

Selvage   Cut Edge

Selvage

Fig. 3-22

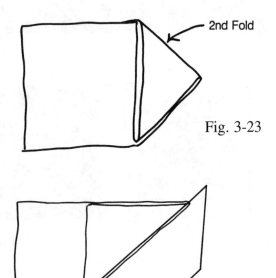

2nd Fold

Fig. 3-23

Fig. 3-24

Cutting Borders and Lattice Strips

1. If you don't mind seams showing periodically throughout the border, cut strips across the fabric and seam them to make one long strip. Then sew them to your quilt.

2. To make an unpieced border, cut strips along the length of your fabric. (The length of the fabric must be at least as long as the border being cut.)

A Few Hints for Cutting

When cutting across seams, check the 90° angle along a seam, **not** an edge. This is much more accurate. If your ruler has cross lines, use them as check-points by placing one on a seam with every cut (Fig. 3-27).

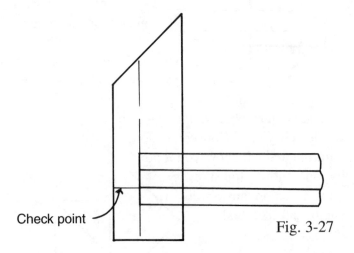

Check point

Fig. 3-27

To cut down on bulk, if stacking multiple layers, stagger seamed units by placing the cut edges parallel to the seams approximately 1/4″ from each other. This will place the seams side by side instead of on top of each other (Fig. 3-28).

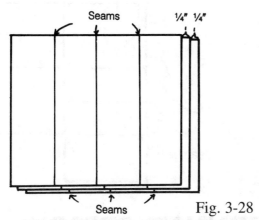

Fig. 3-28

Occasionally, a pattern will require the strips to be cut lengthwise. To do this, open fabric to single thickness and fold selvages back and forth, accordion style (Fig. 3-29). Use first cut to trim selvages away (Fig. 3-30). Cut strips from this edge.

There are several ways to cut borders wider than the width of the ruler.

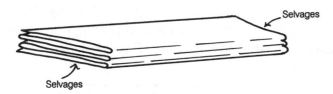

Fig. 3-29

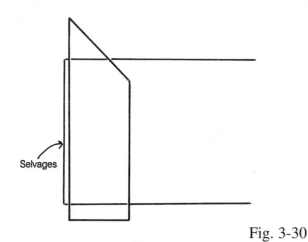

Fig. 3-30

Method 1. Determine the number of extra inches needed and place a square template over that amount. Position ruler next to it and cut (Fig. 3-31).

Caution: Check "excess" measurement across entire width of fabric.

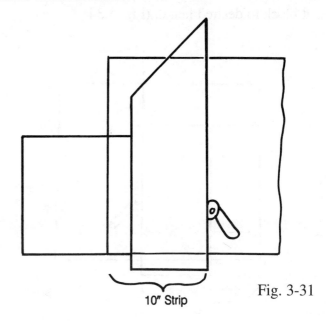

10″ Strip

Fig. 3-31

Method 2. If your mat has grids, line up the folded fabric with a horizontal line, making the first vertical cut at the "0" line on the grid. Place ruler on the grid marking for the border width you need and cut (Fig. 3-32).

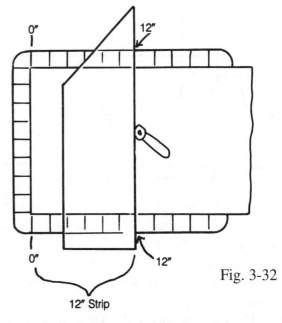

12″ Strip

Fig. 3-32

Method 3. Measure from cut edge and mark at two points. Place ruler on these marks. Cut (Fig. 3-33).

Large blocks can be cut the same way as wide borders. Cut strip the width of the block. If needed, carefully move this strip one-quarter turn on the mat. Cut block to desired length (Fig. 3-34).

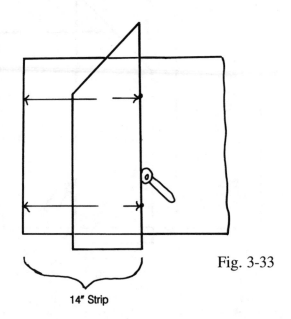

Fig. 3-33

14″ Strip

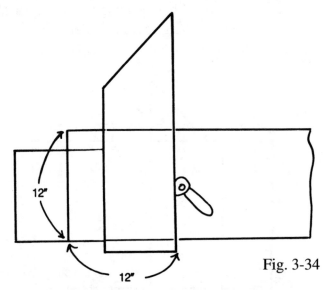

12″

12″

Fig. 3-34

Dress pattern pieces can also be cut with the rotary cutter. Use weights instead of pins. Use a small cutter to manipulate the curves and a ruler for the straight lines. It's easier to cut with the pattern to the left of the ruler when you can. And definitely treat yourself to a big mat for this and a tabletop you can move around, because you can't easily turn the fabric.

Trimming odd and uneven edges from a quilt top is easy with the rotary cutter (Fig. 3-35).

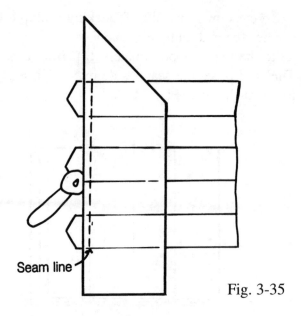

Seam line

Fig. 3-35

DONNA'S SPEEDY SYSTEM

Now that you're an expert at cutting strips, let's move on to shaped pieces. My fast and easy Speedy System consists of simply cutting a stack of strips, then chopping stacks of quilt pieces out of these strips.

Here are the three basic steps:

Step 1. Find or create two parallel lines by simply placing your ruler on one edge and taping the parallel edge. Cut strips to this width (Fig. 3-36).

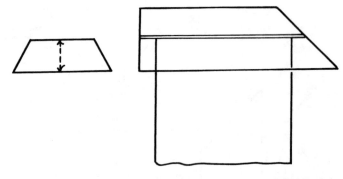

Fig. 3-36

Step 2. Place template over pattern piece. Tape as indicated. You now have:

A. Cutting edges

B. Taped edges; these will be used to match previously cut edges (Fig. 3-37).

Step 3. Use taped template to cut many pieces from stacked strips (Fig. 3-38).

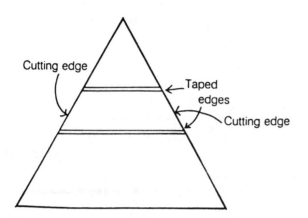

Fig. 3-37

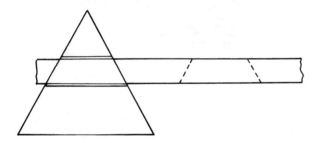

Fig. 3-38

PREPARING TO CUT

Using the Speed-Cutting System

Appendix B offers instruction on rotary-cutting 30 of the most used quilt pattern shapes and their variations. You will, by using and experimenting, quickly learn to recognize them for use in all of your future quilts.

Each page contains the following information:

1. The basic shape of pattern piece (Fig. 3-39).

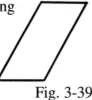

Fig. 3-39

2. Several variations of this piece (the variations are endless!) (Fig. 3-40).

3. Finding or creating the basic strip (Fig. 3-41).

4. Taping and using the basic template (Fig. 3-42).

5. Optional choices of templates (Fig. 3-43).

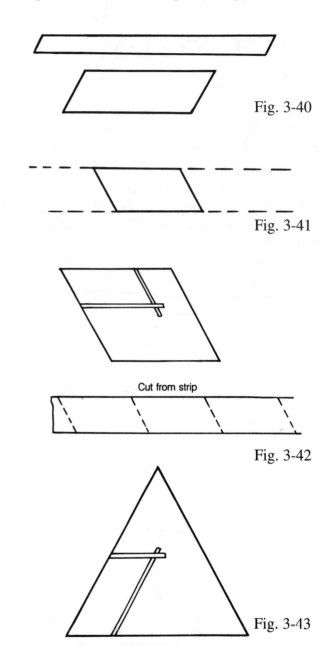

Fig. 3-40

Fig. 3-41

Cut from strip

Fig. 3-42

Fig. 3-43

Taping the Template

1. Choose a template or ruler to fit the shape of the design to be cut. (Pattern must include seam allowances.)

2. Place template on pattern, lining up two outer edges of tool with pattern. Tape all other pattern sides on tool with masking tape. Place tape **around** the pattern, not

inside it. When laying tape down, lean over the table, so you are looking straight down on the pattern.

3. Instructions will refer to the "cutting edge" and the "taped edge" of your template. **All cuts are made on the cutting edges.**

SPEEDY SYSTEM SPECIFICS

The Speedy System instructions are for cutting multiples of a piece. To cut single units, tape template as usual, but instead of starting with a strip, simply cut, rotate, and cut again (Fig. 3-44).

Cutting circular edges is not quite as neat as cutting straight edges. Use the smaller cutter and short, choppy strokes. This allows the layers to ease back in place.

At times you'll need to flip a template over or

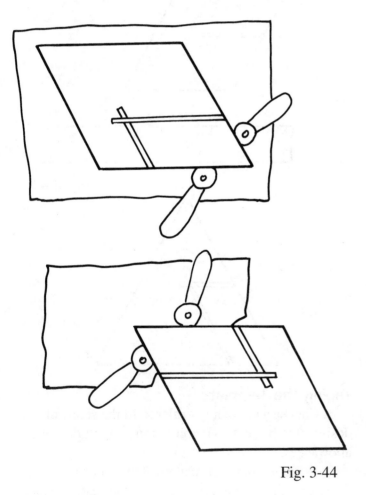

Fig. 3-44

rotate it (Fig. 3-45). This will seem awkward at first, but with a little practice, it will feel very natural.

When cutting small portions from a stack of fabrics, prop the rest of the template on a stack of the same height (Fig. 3-46). Otherwise, your cuts may be inaccurate.

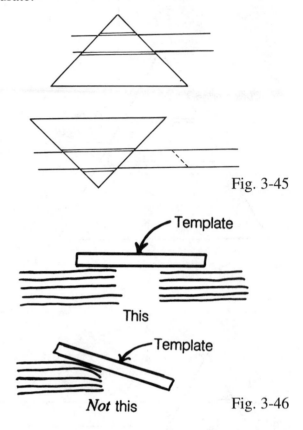

Fig. 3-45

Template

This

Template

Not this   Fig. 3-46

Most pattern pieces can be cut with no regard to layering. However, learn to recognize the following:

1. **"Like" pieces.** Patterns repeat in a "like" fashion (Fig. 3-47). The fabrics must **all** be stacked with right sides up.

2. **"Mirror" pieces.** Patterns repeat in a mirror, or opposite, fashion (Fig. 3-48). The fabrics must be

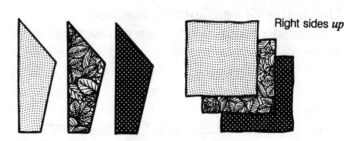

Right sides *up*

Fig. 3-47

stacked with **like sides together**, in the same way as for cutting a garment.

You will still occasionally use scissors. I think of the rotary cutter as the microwave of quilting; even

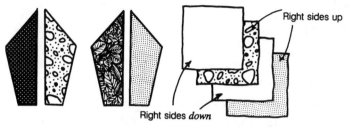

Fig. 3-48

though you own one, you will still sometimes use the range and oven.

A template to be used for a circle or arc for appliqué may be of a slightly different shape than the pattern piece. The unit will assume the correct shape when pressed around the pressing template (Fig. 3-49).

You may, at times, find a curved piece that simply does not match any cutting template. Cut a pattern

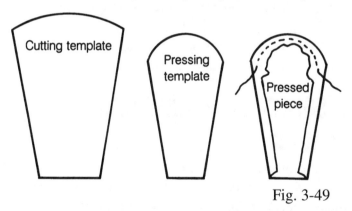

Fig. 3-49

from stiff plastic (available at fabric or quilt stores or by mail order; see Supply List at the end of this book). You can cut three or four layers of fabric with this and the small rotary cutter. You must, however, cut carefully because the blade will easily cut the

plastic. Another option is to draw around this template and cut the three or four layers with scissors.

Angles are often referred to in terms of degrees, and it helps to recognize the shapes. Figure 3-50 shows the most common. A 60°/120° template is not interchangeable with a 45°/90° template, because they are different shapes.

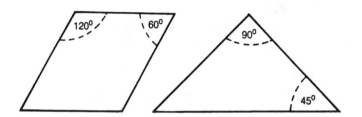

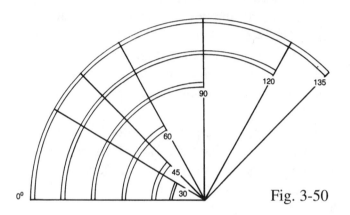

Fig. 3-50

The ruler and templates pictured throughout this book are the Miterite and Speedies from Holiday Designs. Many others can be used. These are simply my personal favorites because they were designed for my Speedy System. Use whatever you are more comfortable with.

Now that you've learned my Speedy System you can cut out any quilt in much less time and more accurately than before! You've really found a way to buy some extra time and pleasure for yourself.

4 PLANNING YOUR QUILT

BASIC CONSTRUCTION PLAN

Step 1. Preparation (covered in this chapter)

A. Choose size, color, and design of quilt.

B. Purchase fabric. Preshrink.

C. Gather all supplies and equipment needed.

Step 2. Cutting

A. Make or tape all cutting templates. Refer to speed-cutting instructions in Chapter 3 as needed.

B. Cut all pieces for quilt top.

Step 3. Sewing

A. Piece center portion of quilt top as instructions indicate. Refer to Chapter 5, Basic Construction Techniques, for specific sewing techniques.

B. Add borders.

Step 4. Finishing

A. Mark quilting lines, if desired.

B. Baste and quilt.

C. Finish edges.

CHOOSING YOUR PROJECT

Now that you've practiced some of these fun and fast techniques, you'll want to use them. Start with one of the 20 quilts in this book. Sound easy? Well, if you're anything like me, you can spend weeks just deciding which one to make first, because you really want to do them all! I try hard to get over that hurdle fast, realizing that in all of that time of indecision, I could have made several quilts.

A FEW HINTS

If you're new to the rotary cutter, start with a quilt labeled "Beginners: Super Easy."

A quilt with one or two pattern pieces is easier and faster to cut out than one with a lot of pieces.

A hand-pieced quilt such as the "Grandmother's Flower Garden" takes longer to stitch. However, it is a great "take-along" project and allows you to be with family and friends while you piece, rather than holed up with your sewing machine.

Special techniques, such as set-ins, curves, six-points, and appliqué, will take a bit longer than straight-line piecing and joining. Of course, this matters only if time is important. If you're enjoying the project, time will seem to pass too quickly, anyhow.

Go with your instincts. If one quilt really jumps out and says, "Do me!," then, do it!

Remember, this is your hobby and if you make your quilts with love and happiness, others will feel it, too.

Once you have chosen which quilt to make, it's time to choose the colors and then the fabrics.

USING THE DESIGN PAGES

Each of the 20 quilts in this book has a design page, which you can use to select colors. Make as many copies of this page as you want. Get a good assortment of colored pencils and some #2 lead pencils. Now start playing with color! You can have hours of fun and you'll be astonished at the many variations you'll come up with!

When you decide which quilt you want to make, cut a copy of the design to the size you want. Copy the borders and add them to the design. This way, you'll have a sketch of the entire quilt.

Border suggestions have been included, but do create your own if you like. Borders can be fun! My favorite is a narrow "framing" strip used as the first border. I use one of my darker fabrics and cut it 1-1/2″ wide (including 1/4″ seam allowance) for small quilts and 2″ wide for medium and large quilts. My last border is usually the widest and always my favorite print from the quilt.

Now count the number of pieces needed of each color and shape. Jot these numbers on a piece of paper, then look up the yardages in Appendix A.

COLOR

Color selection is one of the most important parts of creating a beautiful quilt. It's also the scariest, because the rules we've learned for picking clothing are not the same as for quilts and even the color experts don't agree on the rules! To add to the confusion, some of the most beautiful quilts I've ever seen break all of the rules!

So where in the world is a mere beginner supposed to start? First of all, look in quilt magazines, books, calendars, and at nature for color schemes you like. You'll be surprised at how differently you'll see the world around you.

Ask for help from other quiltmakers, teachers, and store owners. In my classes, we have "show and tell" times to learn how colors and prints work in various combinations. The following are a few guidelines that my students find helpful.

Color Family

First, pick one or two main colors and one or more accent colors. Be flexible, though—you may change your mind when you spot a piece of fabric you "have to have."

An easy way to start is to pick a fabric with the look you want. Study it. Are the colors bright and clear, or grayed earth tones? Whatever the colors, keep all other colors in that family. A bright sailor blue added to a pile of teal, salmon, and taupe will screech like nails across a blackboard. But the same blue with a bright red and sunshine yellow will be terrific.

Look at the proportions of the colors. Which stand out? Which are small highlights? Is the print so small it's almost solid? Is it a bold geometric? A frilly, fussy print?

Use the answers to these questions as a starting point.

When putting fabrics together to create a lovely quilt, there are as many different sets of rules as there are "experts." The soft, subtle quilt that warms

Planning Aunt Sukey's Choice (l. to r.): Dotti, JoAnn, and Josephine.

Sue's heart is simply dull and bland to Nancy. And the bold, vibrating colors Nancy enjoys are garish to Sue.

Color Values

Value is the lightness and darkness of the fabrics. The contrasts and shadings created by the values you choose will determine the character of your quilt.

Fig. 4-1

Look through pages of quilt designs and note the light, medium, and dark values and what they do to the quilts. In general, for a strong, bold look, use high-contrast colors: a very light next to a very dark (your quilt will take on the color of the dark fabric) (Fig. 4-1). For a subdued, quiet look, use low-contrast colors (Fig. 4-2). To create a dark but quiet quilt, use darks and mediums but no lights (Fig. 4-3). For a light but quiet look, use lights, mediums, and no darks (Fig. 4-4).

Fig. 4-2

Fig. 4-3

In a way, there are no mediums. If you put a medium fabric next to a light, there will be a contrast. If you want to soften this contrast, insert fabrics that "shade" the two together.

Fig. 4-4

If you like the look of a particular quilt, it can best be achieved by following the values shown in the graphics, or the photos in the color section. Do feel free to change them, though. Experimenting is fun.

Prints and Stripes

The surest way to achieve an interesting quilt is to use a wide variety of print sizes and styles, including an occasional solid.

For a dramatic, bold look, use all solids. Magnificent quilts are made with a repetition of one or two blocks using two high-contrast solids.

Soft prints and low contrast will produce a lovely, subdued, mellow quilt. (Yes, you can use lots of tiny prints together.)

Cut up large prints at random for an exciting sense of movement. The pieces will not be exactly alike, yet will definitely feel like parts of a whole. Don't be afraid of ending up with headless pheasants and finless fish—you're sure to like the results of experimenting this way.

Don't bother about tiny bits of odd color in a fabric. If you're making a maroon and blue quilt and that perfect navy print has tiny bits of rust in the print, use it. When the quilt is done, your eye will change the rust to maroon.

Some prints create illusions of stripes when viewed from a distance. These usually require no special cutting for small pieces. But for borders and lattice strips, it is important to have the stripe effect line up with the long edge. To achieve this, simply cut these long edges parallel to the selvage and the design will fall right into place.

You may, at times, find a design with areas or motifs you would like to highlight. These will have to be cut individually. (Be sure to buy extra fabric to account for waste.) Be aware of the top and the bottom of this motif in relation to your finished quilt. (The transparent templates are perfect for centering these special prints.)

STAY FLEXIBLE

When you're making a quilt, things happen along the way: you need more of a certain fabric and it's no longer available; the test was wrong and it turned out to be a boy; Aunt Ruth wants a purple quilt and you hate purple. The list is endless.

Relax. Let's consider some alternatives. That fabric you need—could you substitute something close to it? Use a coordinating rather than a matching fabric in the border? Make a lap throw, pillow, or tote bag of this piece and start over on another quilt?

You can give a blue quilt to a baby girl, but people are funny about pink for boys. Put it away for the next girl, choose the quickest quilt in the book, and whip up a new one fast.

You can't picture yourself sewing a whole purple quilt? Try to convince Aunt Ruth that a tiny accent would be much more dramatic than a whole quilt of purple. If you can't get out of it, plan a fast quilt. After all, this should be enjoyable for you, too.

If everything in the project has gone wrong and you just hate it, fold it up neatly, put it in a box, and hide it on the top shelf of a backroom closet. Then forget about it and start something else. A small project that's a guaranteed success will get you quilting again. Someday you'll find that box, and you'll probably find it works this time. If it still doesn't, give it away.

DEVELOPING COLOR SCHEMES YOU'LL LOVE

Select prints because they look good together. The overall design of a fabric will change drastically when cut up in small pieces. A fabric that is ugly on the bolt may be just the thing needed to make your quilt gorgeous.

Black can add excitement (what a shame that we associate it with funerals and villains' hats). Use it to set off brilliant splashes of color. They'll positively vibrate.

Be a little daring if you can. Try an accent of an odd color for a really striking look. Tuck a touch of lavender in a blue quilt, or a bit of teal in a beige piece.

Don't try to coordinate everything. Study nature and you'll see all sorts of color together. Part of the beauty of a forest is the many shades of green in the trees, mixed with the highlights of sun and shadows. A beautiful sunset will include yellow, magenta, brilliant blues, purple, and white. What a magnificent quilt that would make!

After selecting your fabrics, walk away, turn, and take a fast look. Did any stand out? If so, use this as either your main color or in small amounts as a highlight. Did any blend together? Then they'll perform as one fabric and you'll lose the effectiveness of both. Did your fabrics please you? Then, go for it!

And don't ignore your backing fabric. A really smashing print will make your quilt interesting and reversible. If you choose a large print, buy an extra repeat per seam so the design can be easily matched. Rely on your own intuition. It helps to have someone play with the fabrics with you, but for a final choice, you are the one who knows best what you like.

Try not to get a set picture of what your quilt will look like. It's virtually impossible to visualize it as it really will be. Pick fabrics that work well together, then enjoy watching your quilt come to life.

Josephine (l.), JoAnn, and Dotti picking out fabrics.

SCRAP QUILTS

To buy or not to buy? Now there's a question!

Quilters love to save their fabric scraps, but the dilemma of how and when to use them keeps most of these scraps in a closet.

Many of the quilts in this book work very nicely with scraps, so I've included some guidelines to help you get going on what will, undoubtedly, be one of your favorite quilts.

It's easy to get hooked on scrap quilts. They're fun to do, and, best of all, they're fun to use. (A scrap quilt can keep a sick child amused for a long time!)

Once you're hooked, though, you start buying piles of different fabrics to add to your stash so you can make great quilts from this growing pile of "scraps."

The first few of these quilts may be somewhat intimidating. Over the years, I've come up with three guidelines for my own use. Eventually you'll want to make your own list, because scrap quilts are all unique.

1. **Lots of Contrast**. My lights are very light, so that even my mediums become "darks."

2. **Family Unity**. I rarely mix clear, bright colors with gray-tone, earthy colors. It simply doesn't make me feel good. I tend to think of my fabrics as people, and, even though I thoroughly enjoy eccentrics, I do object to a bright red piece screeching its lungs out in the middle of a sedate gathering of soft gray tones.

3. **Don't Over-coordinate**. This is probably the hardest thing to keep from doing in a scrap quilt and really separates the right-brain people from the left-brain!

There is one big drawback in doing scrap quilts: they take a lot of time. You can spend hours just playing with the fabric. The cutting, even with my Speedy System, is slower. Some solutions are:

1. Use quilts with simple pieces such as squares and rectangles.

2. Do quilts with one piece as in "Always Friends" or "Grandmother's Flower Garden."

3. Set up an ongoing scrap quilt. I have a template all taped for "Texas Trellis." Every time I have scraps from something, I cut out six spokes and add them to the box I've set aside for this project. When I sew them together, the cutting and decisions will all be done!

CHARM QUILTS

Anyone who likes scrap quilts will love a charm quilt! They are made with two basic rules:

1. Only one template may be used.

2. Every patch in the entire quilt is a different

fabric than every other patch.

Additional rules seem to differ according to geographical regions.

Last year I completed my first charm quilt and loved every minute of it! You'll find it in this book as the model for the quilt "Always Friends" (see the color section).

Collecting the patches is, in itself, part of the fun. Look to guilds, groups, and magazine ads for opportunities to exchange "charm squares." Fat quarters are fun, too. I've been collecting these for over a year to make a color-coordinated charm quilt in reds, blacks, grays, and whites. I suddenly realized that buying $2.00 pieces of fabric to get one diamond from each is making this the most expensive quilt I'll ever make! But, what the heck—it's been fun.

There are five quilts in this book that would make wonderful charm quilts: Windmill, Grandmother's Flower Garden, Tumbling Blocks, Always Friends, and Clamshell. Try one—you'll be hooked, too!

BUYING THE FABRIC

Now that you've decided on size, layout, and general color scheme, it's time to buy fabric.

One hundred percent cotton is the sturdiest, most durable fabric for quilts. It also has a slight nap, which helps keep the pieces together while stitching.

Buy enough. Fabrics can disappear from a store overnight and may never be available again. Many a quilter has become frustrated and discouraged when she finds that the piece she's run out of is no longer available. Better to buy extra, and if you then have leftovers, you can make marvelous quilts with the scraps.

For this same reason, if you see a fabric you really like, buy it. Manufacturers often produce only one run of a fabric. You may never find it again. How much to buy? My rules of thumb are: (1) if I'm absolutely wild about it, I'll buy at least 2-1/2 yards (enough for an unpieced border); (2) if it's really super background fabric, I'll buy 5 or 6 yards; and (3) if it's a nice accent piece, but a little goes a long way, I'll get 1 or 2 yards.

If stripes are used in your quilt, consider the waste. You'll need 1/4 to 1/2 yard or more extra fabric.

The yardages in this book are based on 44" fabric and allow extra for shrinkage and waste.

Store fabric neatly, preferably in boxes and according to color. I like those open plastic crates because you can see the fabric from all sides. Avoid airtight plastic bags, which will eventually cause your fabric to deteriorate.

Trying out different layouts with Susan's Love Ring (l. to r.): Brenda, Susan, Barbara, and Connie.

PREPARING YOUR FABRIC FOR QUILTING

Prewashing is recommended to preshrink the fabric and remove excess sizing. The grain is then reliable just as it comes from the dryer. It has the extra advantage of washing out any excess dye from the darker fabrics, and you'll have a washable quilt when finished.

Test medium and dark fabrics to be sure they won't run when washed again. I do this by wetting a corner of the fabric, then squeezing it between two white paper towels. If the towels remain white, I consider the piece colorfast. If it bleeds, I'll rinse it until the water runs clear. If there is still bleeding after four or five rinses, I will actually discard that fabric! It is not worth ruining a quilt with it.

Snip a little 1/4" triangle off each of the four corners of your fabric before tossing it in the washing machine. This cuts down on raveling and tangling. Wash lights and darks separately.

Try a light spray of fabric sizing when ironing—

it's much easier to get the wrinkles out. It also adds a bit more body, making all of those small pieces easier to work with. If you're working with a lot of bias cuts, this is a "must."

SUPPLIES

The following supplies are quite common in today's quilting scene. Ask for them at your local sewing or quilting store. If they do not stock an item, perhaps they can order it for you. If you are not close to a store, look in the Supply List at the back of this book. I have included a list of fine mail-order sources there.

Rotary Cutting Equipment. See Chapter 2 for more information.

Fabric. 100% cotton. Fabric purchasing and preparation are discussed in detail earlier in this chapter.

1/4″ Quilter's Tape. A narrow, low-residue tape to use on your cutting templates.

Template Plastic. Used in cutting Double Wedding Ring

Fine, Permanent Marking Pen. For marking on template plastic. My favorite is the Pigma Pen because it can be used to write on muslin, too.

Spray Starch. Helps on any fabrics that lose their body after laundering.

Long, Large Head Quilting Pins. You won't know how you lived without them!

Silk Pins. These are long, extra-fine dressmaker pins that glide easily through your fabric.

Sequin Pins. Many of my students prefer these very short pins for appliqué.

Safety Pins. Nickel-plated, 1″ long; about 350 will baste a double-bed-size quilt.

Sewing Thread. My favorite is a large cone of natural colored thread. I wind a dozen bobbins with it and I'm set for hours. You may use odds and ends of good quality thread for piecing, because it does not have to match the fabric. You will also need thread to match backing fabric (for machine-quilting only) and to match outer border (which in some quilts becomes the binding).

Fine Sewing Thread. Silk or silk-finish for hand appliqué. Must match or blend with the fabric.

Pearl Cotton #3. Only for tying quilts; it has sheen, is washable, and is easy to handle. Use two or three strands.

Invisible Thread. Machine-quilting only.

Quilting Thread. Hand-quilting only.

Quilting Needles. Hand-quilting only. Use "betweens" size 8 to 10; the smaller the needle, the shorter the stitch!

Hand Sewing Needle. For appliqué and hand sewing, use sharps or milliners, size 10.

Large Darning Needle or **Curved Upholstery Needle**. For tying quilts.

Lightweight Cardboard. Use as pressing templates. Any of the following will work: manila folders, index cards, poster board, or cereal boxes.

Walking Foot or **Even-feed Foot**. Machine-quilting only. It will feed the three thicknesses of your quilt evenly.

Darning Foot. Machine-quilting only. Use for free-form quilting.

Common Sewing Tools. Scissors, seam ripper, thimble, etc. No list here, because everyone has her favorites.

Thimble. Try them all until you find one you like. It will be worth the effort.

Iron. I prefer a steam iron used gently.

Quilting Stencils. Use to draw quilting lines on quilt. Purchase these or create your own from light-weight plastic sheets.

Marking Pen (Water Soluble). Needed only to mark quilting lines. If all of your quilting follows seamlines, this is not needed.

Batting. Look for the word "bonded." It holds up well in the washing machine and needs very little quilting.

Flannel or **Fleece**. Often used as batting for clothing or table coverings. Wash flannel several times to preshrink thoroughly before using.

Lap Frame. Only for hand-quilting small areas at a time.

Hoop or Floor Frame. Only for hand-quilting whole quilts.

Bicycle Clips. Hold quilt tightly rolled for machine-quilting.

Quilt Label. Sign your quilt. Tell the world you're proud of it!

5 BASIC CONSTRUCTION TECHNIQUES

SEWING SKILLS

My beginning students always ask, "How do I know when to rip it out?" I tell them the following:

Be as accurate as you can while still having fun. Remember, this is your hobby, not your job, and your first quilts will not be museum-quality pieces, so don't spend time ripping out every seam that's not a perfect match. If you enjoy your first quilt, you'll make more of them, and as you do, you'll get better at it.

If you need to do some easing to get seams to match, don't worry. The quilting takes up a lot of errors in the "puffies."

Know what is really important and pay attention to that. For example, learn to maintain a scant 1/4″ seam allowance. Careful cutting is important. Learn to adjust your sewing machine to maintain good tension. Use a small size (70/10) sewing machine needle for machine-piecing, and change it every time you start a new quilt. Use good quality fabrics and thread.

Pay attention to these things and you'll be amazed at how easily it all fits together!

MACHINE-PIECING

A balanced tension is important. Your stitching should not draw up the fabric (if it does, your tension is too tight or your stitches too long). You should not see the bobbin thread from the top side.

For piecing, use a medium to small stitch (12-15 stitches per inch). There is no backstitching at the end of most of the seams, and these small stitches will not pull out.

Use a fine to medium machine needle size (70/10 to 80/12). **Change the needle often**; it will make a difference in the quality of your stitching.

Poke through your box of machine accessories and find the single-hole needle plate (Fig. 5-1) to replace that wide hole (zigzag) plate. You'll have better control of your fabric with the single-hole plate. Don't set your machine on zigzag. If you don't have a single-hole needle plate, decenter the needle to the left or right, but remember that doing so changes the width of your seam allowance. Or tape an index card over the zigzag needle plate, cutting holes for the feed dogs. Lower an unthreaded needle into the card. Then enlarge the hole slightly.

Fig. 5-1

THE 1/4″ SEAM

Finding and maintaining a perfect 1/4″ seam will make your piecing time enjoyable. Pieces fit together; ripping is almost nonexistent. To find a reference point on your sewing machine, mark a line 1/4″ from the edge of a piece of paper. Insert the machine needle into the line. Drop the presser foot. Find an easy sighting at the edge of the paper (the edge of the foot, the presser foot opening, etc.). You may want to use masking tape or a seam guide. On some machines, you can decenter the needle so that the needle falls 1/4″ away from any sighting you choose. If you have a computerized machine, make sure you return to this setting every time you turn on the machine again. Learn to guide the cut edge of your fabric along this sighting, and you won't have to spend time marking your seams.

About that 1/4″ seam—make it a scant 1/4″ (Fig. 5-2). There's a bit of loft in the fabric at any seam, creating a shortage in the size of that piece. It may seem insignificant, but a block with eight pieced seams can end up much shorter than a block with only two seams. Using scant 1 / 4 ″ s e a m s allows for this loft (Fig. 5-3).

Fig. 5-2

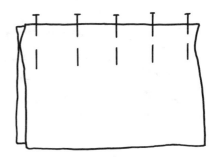

Fig. 5-3   Loft

A good way to test for accuracy is to sew three 2″ wide strips together. Press the seams all to one side. If the unit measures exactly 5″ wide, your seams are perfect! If not, try again until you've got it. This little exercise is worth it.

TO PIN OR NOT TO PIN

There are people who would refuse to sew if they had to pin. Others create metal sculptures of their seams. The majority of us use pins only at key places.

In general, a few well-placed pins help on any bias seam, set-in blocks, eight-point stars, long seams, and matched seams.

Pin across seams (Fig. 5-4), but always remove a pin before the needle comes to it. Sewing across pins is hard on your needle, weakens the seam, and shifts the fabric at that point.

Fig. 5-4

Josephine (l.), Susan, and Sarah laying-out Grandmother's Flower Garden.

SEWING LONG STRIPS TOGETHER

To sew strips evenly without pinning, match up one end of the strips, sew two stitches, and stop with the needle **in** the fabric. Without stretching, match the edges of the next 12-20″. Hold tightly at this point and, pulling slightly, stitch. Stop and repeat to the end of the seam.

If you simply allow the two pieces to feed through without doing this, the two strips will be uneven, causing the unit to curve (Fig. 5-5).

When sewing three or more strips, alternate the sewing direction to prevent the strips from curving (Fig. 5-6).

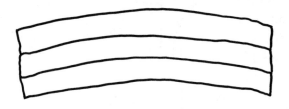

Fig. 5-5

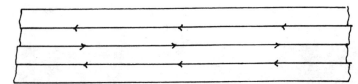

Fig. 5-6

MATCHING SEAMS

1. Always press matching seams in opposite directions (Fig. 5-7).

2. For perfect matching, pin seams together at the seam line. Stitch up to the pin before removing.

3. With practice, most seams can be matched quite nicely by butting them together with your fingers and holding them as close as possible while stitching.

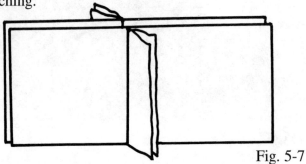

Fig. 5-7

EASING

Don't be alarmed if occasionally you need to ease two pieces together. Just pin the two ends in place and **gently** pull the fabric as it is sewn. If possible, sew with the larger piece against the feed dogs. (If the two pieces simply don't fit, check to make sure you've cut them from the correct templates.) Note: If sewing bias to bias, **never** pull to ease. "Pat" them in place instead.

SET-INS

(Pieces joined to an inside corner)

1. Sew each side of the set-in piece as two separate seams.

2. Stitch each seam away from the inside corner.

3. The first seam is sewn with the set-in piece on the bottom (Fig. 5-8). The first stitch should meet the end stitch of the adjoining seam. Backstitch two or three stitches.

4. The second seam is sewn with the set-in piece on top (Fig. 5-9). The first stitch should meet the first stitch of the first seam. Backstitch two or three stitches.

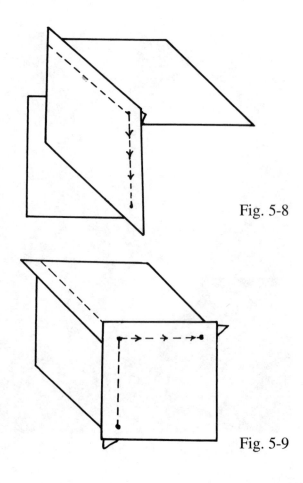

Fig. 5-8

Fig. 5-9

JOINING EIGHT-POINTS

1. Sew four sets of two pieces each (Fig. 5-10).

2. Press and join as shown. If sewing bias pieces (as in eight-point stars), be very careful not to stretch the seams or edges.

3. Join and press these units as shown. Trim extending corners at joining points (Fig. 5-11).

4. Insert pin straight through both pieces at point where all seams meet (Fig. 5-12). Holding this pin straight out, pin 1/8″ on either side of center point, as illustrated. Remove center pin (Fig. 5-13).

5. When sewing a long seam it is helpful to stabilize the center so the pins can be removed (Fig. 5-14).

6. When stitching the seam be careful not to stretch the fabric. Sew over the pins slowly, gently pushing heavy thicknesses under the machine foot (Fig. 5-15). (Yes, I know I said don't sew over pins, but this is an exception.)

7. Press seam to one side. If center does not lie flat, try steam pressing it. Don't be alarmed at a little wrinkling because it will probably quilt out. But if the center still stands up a bit, restitch it, making a deeper seam at the center point.

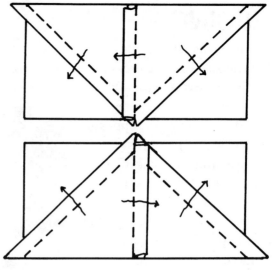

Fig. 5-11

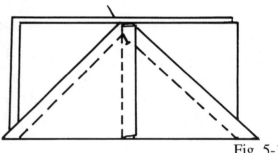

Fig. 5-12

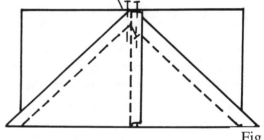

Fig. 5-13

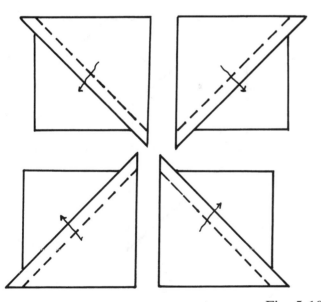

Fig. 5-10

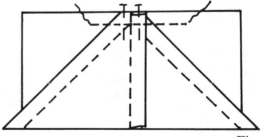

Fig. 5-14

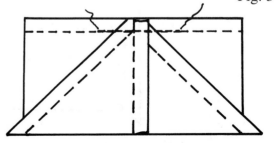

Fig. 5-15

PRESSING

1. Never press seams open; always press to one side. Whenever possible, press the seams toward the darker fabric. **Exception:** When one seam will be matched to another, press them in opposite directions (Fig. 5-7).

2. To position the seams, press very lightly on the underside first. Press with or without steam, as you prefer, but steam can change the size and shape of a piece, so use it with caution.

3. Press on the right side, sliding the iron gently across the seam while using your free hand underneath to position the seams. Move the iron in the same direction you're pressing the seam. Resist the urge to pull at any point on your fabric! Press gently. You are not ironing a pair of blue jeans.

How do I match these points? JoAnn (l.), Barbara, and Brenda.

ANGLES AND POINTS

After a while, you will become quite good at judging 1/4″ areas. But until then, you may want to mark a few corners with 1/4″ seams (remember: scant). The following are the most difficult to judge:

1. Sewing two different angles (Fig. 5-16).

2. Sewing any seam that must end 1/4″ from the edge, as for set-ins (Fig. 5-17).

3. Matching two angled seams (Fig. 5-18).

Note: There are a number of items available to help with this. Look for them in your quilt shops and catalogs.

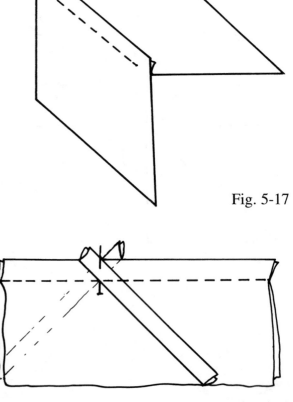

Fig. 5-17

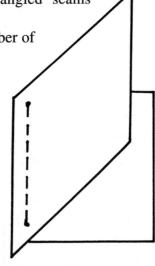

Fig. 5-16

Fig. 5-18

SEWING CURVES

1. Pin pieces at center point of seam (Fig. 5-19). Short curves can be done by sight. On longer curves, fold the pieces in half to find the centers.

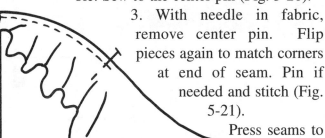

Fig. 5-19

2. With the concave (outer) curve on top, flip the pieces apart so the starting corners can be matched and held together. Pin if it helps. Take two stitches and stop with the needle in the fabric. Gathering the excess fabric in your left hand, gently line up the raw edges of the two pieces. Try not to stretch the bottom piece if possible. Sew to the center pin (Fig. 5-20).

3. With needle in fabric, remove center pin. Flip pieces again to match corners at end of seam. Pin if needed and stitch (Fig. 5-21).

Fig. 5-20

Press seams to outer curve (Fig. 5-22). There is no need to clip curved seams on a quilt because the puckery look will be absorbed in the quilting. This is wonderful. As much as I like the Love Ring, I'd never make one if I had to clip all of those little seams.

Fig. 5-21

Fig. 5-22

"FACTORY" METHOD

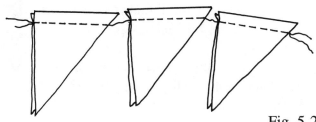

Fig. 5-23

When sewing several identical units, feed them through the machine without separating them (Fig. 5-23). This method is faster and makes it easier to keep your pieces in order. Later you can clip them apart.

Chain-piecing, factory method (l. to r.): Brenda and Linda.

HAND-PIECING WITH NO MARKED SEAM LINES

Hand-piecing is becoming quite popular again, because it makes quilting a portable hobby and one that's soothing to the nerves. But drawing seam lines on the pieces is time-consuming and does terrible things to bias edges. So I devised a method of training yourself to hand-piece perfect 1/4″ seams by sight.

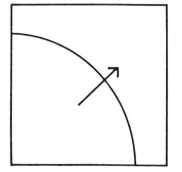

All you do is mark the first few seams. Then start making these marks lighter and lighter until you only **think** you can see them. Now try it with no marks, and you'll find you've trained your eye to see the 1/4″ mark. Give it a try—it really works!

Using a #10 milliner's needle (or your own favorite) and a fine quality sewing thread, sew a tiny running stitch 1/4″ (scant, see page 31) from edges. Try for 16-18 stitches per inch. Evenness matters.

Sew only to the seam ends, leaving all seam allowances free. Backstitch at the beginning and end of all seams (Fig. 5-24).

When moving to an adjacent seam, take the needle through seam allowances at the **exact** point where the seams meet. Continue stitching.

Hand-piecing Grandmother's Flower Garden—with no stitching lines—are Linda (l.) and Brenda.

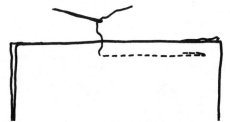

Fig. 5-24

HAND APPLIQUÉ

There are many techniques for doing hand appliqué. You may want to explore them and choose the one you prefer. The following is a simple, basic hand appliqué technique that I like.

Step 1. Make a pressing template out of lightweight cardboard. I use old manila folders and index cards. Poster board and cereal boxes are good, too. (Template plastic won't work because the iron will melt it.)

Use dressmaker's carbon to trace the shape on the cardboard. Pressing templates should **not** include the seam allowances on the edges to be appliquéd. Do not add them.

Step 2. Cut out the appliqué shapes with a rotary cutter. Edges with an inward curve will need to be clipped at several points. Clips should be slightly **less** than 1/4″ (Fig. 5-25).

Fig. 5-25

Step 3. For shapes with curved edges, take a small running stitch 1/8″ in from the cut edge. Leave about 1″ of thread at each end (Fig. 5-26). Stitch the outer edge of each arc separately.

Place the cardboard template 1/4″ from the cut edge. Gently pull the running stitch taut (Fig. 5-27). Press edges over cardboard with a steam iron. Remove template. Leave the running stitch in. It can be used later, if needed, to pull the seam back in place.

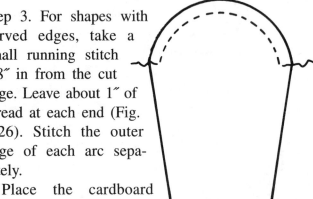

Fig. 5-26

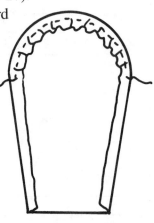

Fig. 5-27

To create sharp points, clip excess fabric to 1/4″ from the point. Fold down on template (Fig. 5-28). Fold points along template edge (Fig. 5-29). Fold seam allowances in. Press (Fig. 5-30).

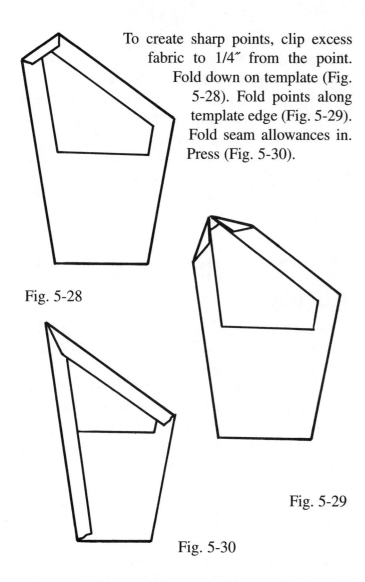

Fig. 5-28

Fig. 5-29

Fig. 5-30

Step 4. Pin or baste piece in place. For fine appliqué stitches:

Use a #10 or #12 sharp sewing needle.

Use fine sewing thread, either silk or silk-finish. To prevent twisting while sewing, use the thread in the direction it comes off the spool (Fig. 5-31).

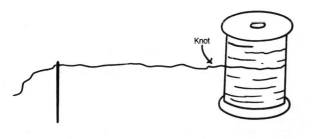

Knot

Fig. 5-31

For almost invisible stitches, take a small stitch in the background fabric. As you come up, catch just

two or three threads of the fold of the appliqué piece (Fig. 5-32).

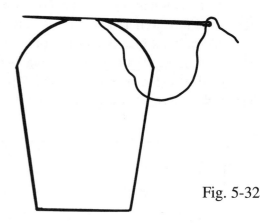

Fig. 5-32

Start the next background stitch as close as possible to the stitch taken in the fold.

MACHINE "HAND APPLIQUÉ"

An easy, fast method of achieving the fine look of hand appliqué is zigzagging over the edges with invisible thread (Fig. 5-33).

Step 1. Set sewing machine to narrow zigzag or blind hem stitch, matching the length and width shown (Fig. 5-34).

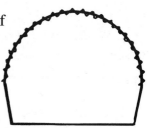

Fig. 5-33

Fig. 5-34

Step 2. Lower upper tension slightly so the bobbin thread does not show on top.

Step 3. Start and stop with 1/2″ of very tight stitches (Fig. 5-35). Stitch in a continuous unbroken line as much as possible.

½″   ½″

Fig. 5-35

HANDLING BIAS

Next to maintaining a scant 1/4″ seam, handling bias is the most ignored key to easy piecing.

1. Learn what bias is and form the habit of being aware of it: **straight grain** is the two directions (lengthwise and crosswise) of the threads used to weave the fabric. Bias is any other direction. **True**

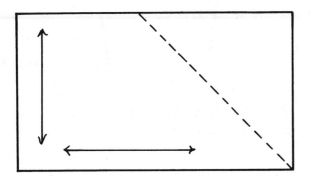

Fig. 5-36

bias is a 45° angle to the straight grain (Fig. 5-36).

2. When sewing a bias edge to a straight edge, try to sew with the bias piece on the bottom. If it's on top, your machine foot will stretch it by pushing the fabric ahead.

3. When pressing a piece with a bias edge, either set the iron down and pick it up without moving it, or gently move the iron **with the grain** of the bias piece (Fig. 5-37).

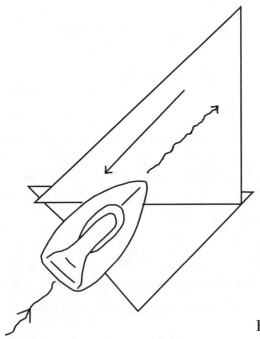

Fig. 5-37

4. All pressing should be done on the topside to eliminate pleats. Use your free hand to position seams underneath. Do not pull or stretch fabric.

5. If you've prewashed a fabric that will be cut up into triangles, diamonds, or other bias shapes, use a spray-on fabric sizing when ironing it.

6. As your project grows in size and weight, learn to handle it flat or folded, rather than picking it up at a raw edge. Otherwise, the weight of the quilt will stretch any unstitched bias edges.

RECOGNIZING GRAIN OF FABRIC

There will be times when you must sew the bias edge of a shape that appears to have identical edges. Which is the bias edge?

Of course, you could easily tell which is the bias edge by stretching it, but then you'd ruin the piece. Learn to "see" the threads of your fabric and you'll begin to recognize bias edges without even thinking about it.

Start by closely examining a light-colored piece of fabric. You'll see tiny lines running in two directions. You're seeing the threads that were used to weave the fabric. The direction of these threads is the straight grain. Lengthwise grain refers to the long threads first laid in the weaving loom. These threads are taut, allowing no "give." Crosswise grain refers to the threads that are woven back and forth across the fabric. They run from selvage to selvage (the woven edge of the fabric) (Fig. 5-38). Pull in this direction and you'll feel the difference from the lengthwise grain. The fabric "gives" quite a bit! This is why some patterns specify the pieces are to be cut on the lengthwise grain.

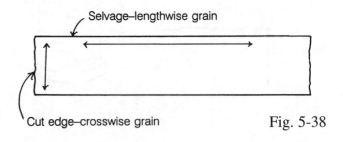

Selvage–lengthwise grain

Cut edge–crosswise grain

Fig. 5-38

SEWING THE QUILT TOP BLOCKS TOGETHER

If space allows, lay all of the blocks out on the floor (or table) before sewing. Stack the first two columns in order, keeping the top block of the quilt on the top of the stack (Fig. 5-39). Sew the two top squares together (part of row 1). **Without cutting the thread**, sew the next two squares together (part of row 2). Continue in this manner until the entire stack is sewn (Fig. 5-40).

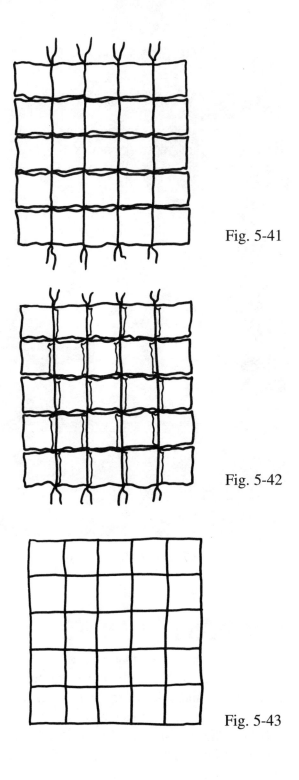

Fig. 5-41

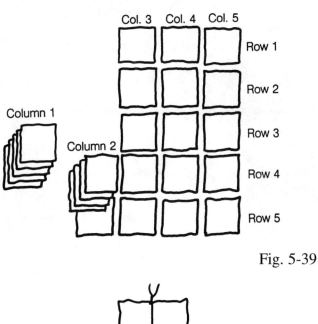

Fig. 5-39

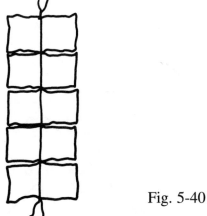

Fig. 5-40

Fig. 5-42

Fig. 5-43

Stack column three and, starting at the top, sew the squares to column two. Continue adding columns until all vertical seams have been completed (Fig. 5-41).

Press seams on alternating rows to the left. Press remaining seams to the right (Fig. 5-42).

Stitch horizontal seams (Fig. 5-43). Press all in the same direction.

A modern quilting bee! Front (l. to r.): Sarah and Linda; back (l. to r.): Susan, Josephine, JoAnn, Connie, Barbara, Brenda, and Dotti.

ON-POINT QUILTS

On-point quilts are made up of squares that are turned so the corners of the block are pointing to the top, bottom, and sides of the quilt. This leaves triangular areas along the edges and corners that must be filled in. The easiest method is the floating version. In this, the triangles are cut slightly larger than needed (Fig. 5-44). As one row is sewn to another, the seam simply extends across this excess fabric. When finished, the blocks appear to be floating on the background.

To prepare the side triangles of the quilt, cut a square in half diagonally to make two triangles. The diagonal edges will be on the bias grain. They are set into the quilt with these bias edges surrounding the quilt, which means they can be steamed and eased later if needed.

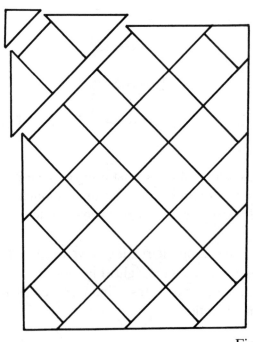

Fig. 5-44

But they could also stretch while you're working. To keep from stretching this bias, I recommend the following steps:

1. Fold square in half. Press (Fig. 5-45).
2. Staystitch 1/4″ on each side of the fold (Fig. 5-46).
3. Coat lightly with spray starch. When dry, cut pieces apart (Fig. 5-47).

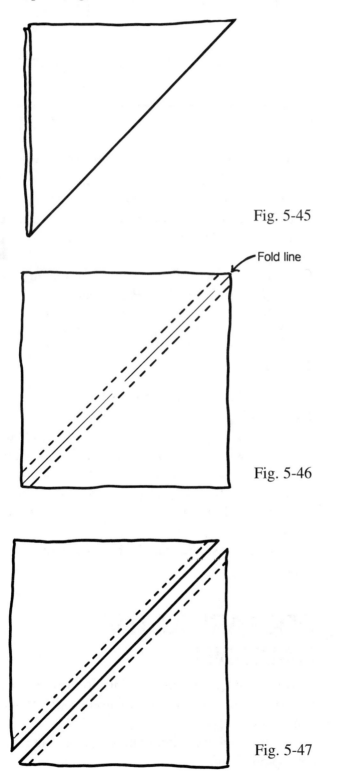

Fig. 5-45

Fig. 5-46

Fig. 5-47

BORDERS

First Border Only

Lay entire pieced center on a flat surface. Without stretching, lay the two ends of the first border down the center of the length of the quilt. Cut. Pin one border to each side edge, right sides together, easing the quilt to fit, if needed. Stitch (Fig. 5-48). Attach end pieces in same manner (Fig. 5-49).

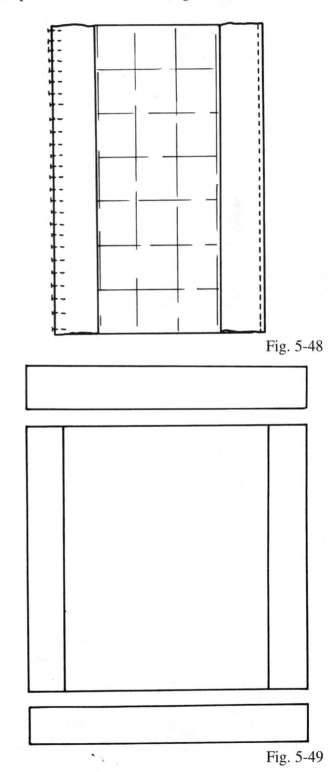

Fig. 5-48

Fig. 5-49

Remaining Borders

Remaining borders should not require measuring and pinning, but are otherwise added in the same sequence.

Mitering Borders: Speedy Method

Step 1. Sew border strips to sides. Backstitch at beginning and end of each seam. Leave seam allowances at ends free. Place short lengthwise edge of Miterite against border seam line as shown. Draw along angled edge (seam line) (Fig. 5-50).

Step 2. Move seam line guide of Miterite over line drawn in Step 1. Draw along angled edge as shown (cutting line) (Fig. 5-51). Repeat on all corners. Sew right sides together, on seam lines (Fig. 5-52). Trim along cutting line.

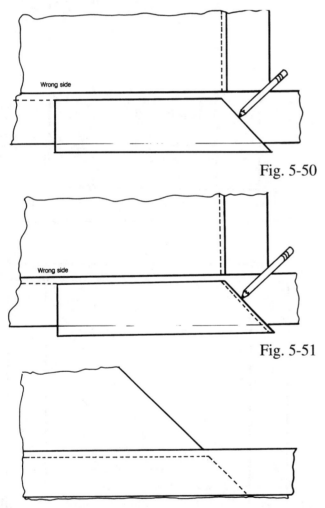

Fig. 5-50

Fig. 5-51

Fig. 5-52

Mitering Borders: Traditional Method

1. Sew borders to quilt, centering each strip on the quilt edge. Border strips should extend equal amounts on both ends. Stitching must stop 1/4″ from quilt edge end. Backstitch to secure.

2. With wrong side up, gently smooth the left border over the right one. Draw a diagonal line from the inner seam to the point where outer edges cross (Fig. 5-53).

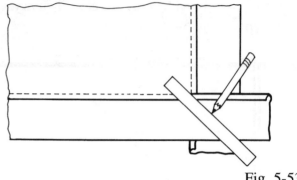

Fig. 5-53

3. Fold quilt, right sides together, until adjacent border edges are lined up with each other (Fig. 5-52). Stitch along diagonal line, stitching from outer edge to inner seam. Do not catch original border seams. Backstitch.

4. Check corner shape; it should form a 90° corner. Trim seams to 1/2″. Press open.

MARKING THE QUILT TOP

Any marking of quilting lines should be done just before basting.

If your quilting is to follow a seam line or appliqué edge, you will not need to mark it. For designs in open areas, use a washable marker or chalk pencil. (Marks made with a lead pencil do not wash out.) Mark very lightly. This is nicer to quilt and easier to remove.

Be sure to test any markers on a scrap of the same fabric first.

PREPARING THE BACKING

Wash and iron backing fabric. Remove selvages. Cut and seam (1/2″ seams) as needed. Press seams open.

The finished back should be at least 2″ bigger than the top on all sides.

BASTING THE QUILT

You'll need a large, flat surface to work on. Mark the center of this surface and the center of your quilt backing. Matching these centers, lay the quilt backing **wrong side up** on the table. Center the batting on top of the backing. Center the quilt top, right side up, on the batting.

To be sure there are no folds or wrinkles on the bottom, pull gently on each of the four sides of the backing fabric. Repeat this every time you reposition the quilt during the basting process. If using a cotton or part-cotton batting, tape the entire backing to an uncarpeted surface. Check with a community center or church—many will allow you to use their tables and floor space for this.

Starting at the center and working out, pin through all layers, using 1″ long, nickel-plated safety pins. Position pin every 3-4″ (Fig. 5-54). Avoid placing any pins directly on a line to be quilted.

When the entire area on top of the table has been basted, carefully slide the quilt so an unbasted area is now on top. Repeat until quilt is completely basted.

Check the underside for pleats and wrinkles. You may want to rebaste an area.

Pin-basting the Six-Point Star (l. to r.): Connie, Dotti, Linda, and Sarah.

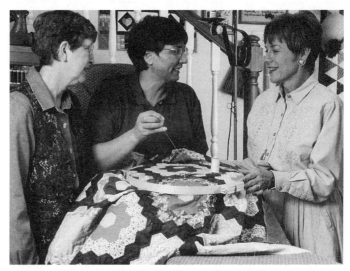

Hand-quilting Grandmother's Flower Garden (l. to r.): Barbara, Sarah, and Linda.

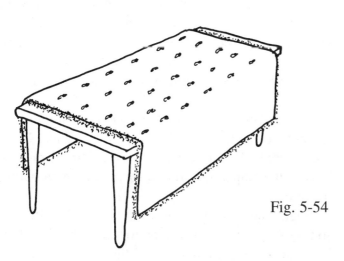

Fig. 5-54

HAND-QUILTING

Hand-quilting is basically a running stitch holding the three layers together. You'll need quilting thread, short needles called "betweens" (#8 is easiest to learn with, but #10 will give you shorter stitches), a thimble (you'll need one; there are all kinds of thimbles and variations available today, so keep trying until you find something you can work with), and some sort of frame. Start with a lap frame or hoop. If you enjoy it you may want to check out the floor frames available.

The stitch requires practice. Start with a tiny knot. Enter the fabric about 1″ from the first quilting stitch. Snap the thread just hard enough to pull the knot through the top layer, catching it in the batting (Fig. 5-55).

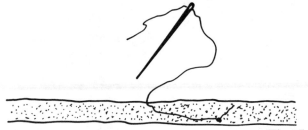

Fig. 5-55

With your free hand underneath the quilt, insert the needle straight down (Fig. 5-56). As soon as your finger feels the point, "rock" the needle down, at the same time pushing the point up.

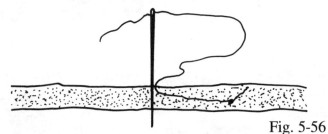

Fig. 5-56

Repeat these two motions, using your thumb (upper hand) to push the fabric over the point (Fig. 5-57).

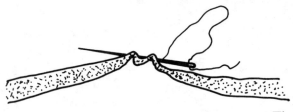

Fig. 5-57

To end the thread, take one or two tiny back-stitches, then come out about 1″ away, and cut thread short, leaving a 1″ tail end anchored in the batting.

With today's bonded batting, it is not as important to get tiny stitches. Try first to get **even** stitches, then try for shorter ones, if you wish.

HINTS FOR MACHINE-QUILTING

Machine-quilting is even easier today because of the walking foot (or even-feed foot) and transparent thread.

When quilting over two or more colors of fabric,

Machine-quilting sure is faster! Shown is Linda Crabtree.

use a clear thread on the top. You'll need to loosen the top tension to get a perfect stitch. For the bobbin, choose a good sewing thread to match the backing fabric.

With a walking foot, you will not have to push or pull the quilt through the machine. Be careful, however, that the weight of the quilt does not create a drag.

Where to quilt is personal. Most people pick out specific seam lines and follow them. Your movement is limited when you are machine-quilting a large item, so you'll need to choose your quilting lines with this in mind. There are attachments available, however, that allow a free movement of the fabric while stitching. You may want to experiment with these. (See the Bibliography for several good books on machine-quilting.)

For machine-quilting, use a longer stitch (6-8 stitches per inch). It feeds through easier and has a puffier look. If you're using a clear thread on top, loosen the upper tension to keep the thread from breaking.

Begin and end stitching lines with 1/2″ of stitches so tiny that they are almost on top of each other. This holds the invisible thread better than backstitching.

The trick to machine-quilting is to learn how to handle bulk. Roll each side tightly toward the center quilting line. Bicycle clips help keep these two rolls in place (Fig. 5-58). Fold as shown to make a manageable bundle to put in your lap (Fig. 5-59). Using a walking foot and a long machine stitch, sew the entire length of this quilting line. Reroll the quilt to the next area and stitch. Repeat until quilt is done.

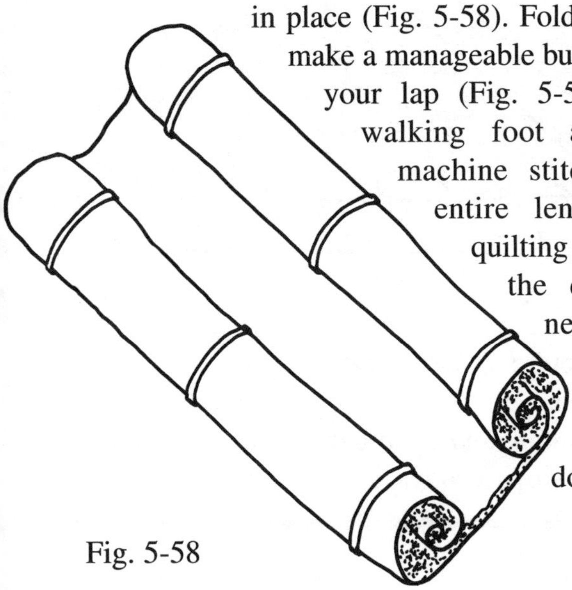

Fig. 5-58

Fig. 5-59

TYING A QUILT

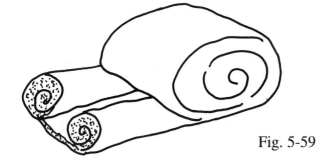

This is the fastest way to finish a quilt. Follow the same procedure for basting, but instead of pinning, tie it.

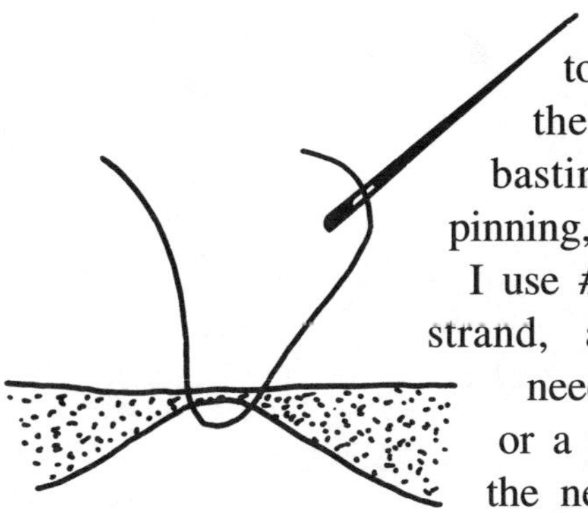

I use #3 pearl cotton, double strand, and a large darning needle. You'll need pliers or a piece of rubber to pull the needle through. Using a long piece of thread (about 36″ when doubled), take one stitch

Fig. 5-60

Fig. 5-61

through all layers (Fig. 5-60). Knot this by tying it just twice (Fig. 6-61).

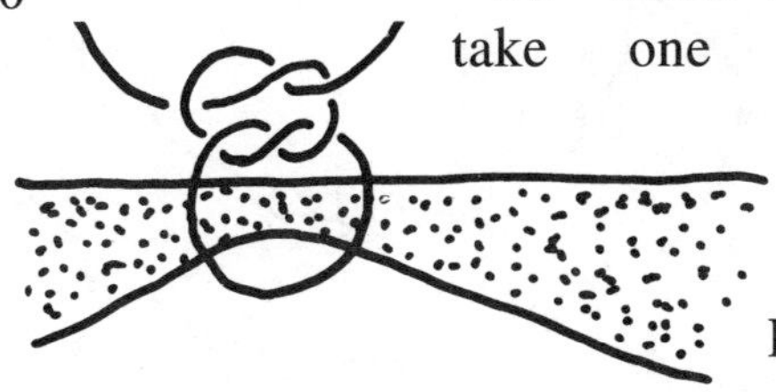

You'll gather the quilt at the tied spot, but don't worry, it will work out as it's used. Cut the tail ends 1″ long and go on to the next one.

Tied quilts have very little quilting, so you'll need a batting that stays together under these conditions. Use either bonded batting, flannel fabric, or a flannel sheet.

BINDING THE EDGES

Binding the edges is the last step in creating a quilt. The quickest way is to turn the raw edge of the outer border to the back and stitch it in place. To do this the outer border must be cut 1-1/2″ wider than the finished width, allowing 1-1/4″ for turnback. (All outer borders in this book include that extra width.)

1. With right sides up, trim off excess batting and backing so all edges are even with outer border edge (Fig. 5-62).

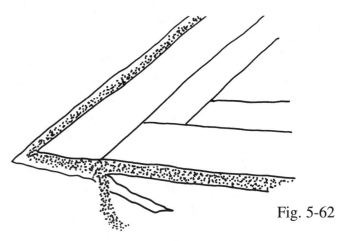

Fig. 5-62

2. With back sides of quilt up, trim 1″ off backing and batting (Fig. 5-63). **(Do not cut off any border fabric.)**

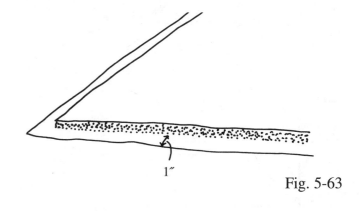

1″

Fig. 5-63

3. Turn 1-1/4″ of border to the back of the quilt. You will be turning back 1/4″ of the batting/backing also. This is necessary to retain a plump binding when quilt is used. Turn under 1/4″ of raw edge. Pin. Machine-stitch.

4. For easy mitered corners, fold corner wrong side out, as shown (Fig. 5-64). Measure 1-3/4″ from point. Mark or pin.

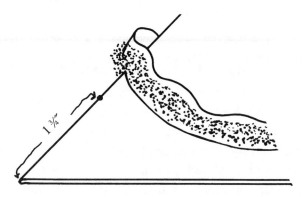

1 3/4″

Fig. 5-64

5. Fold point at mark, keeping cut edges together. Mark quilt at fold line (Fig. 5-65). Stitch 1-1/4″ from fold. Backstitch. Trim seam to 1/2″, tapering at corner (Fig. 5-66). Turn to right side. Mitered corner will fall neatly in place, leaving 1/4″ free to turn under (Fig. 5-67).

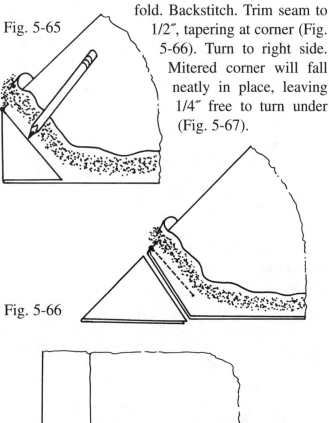

Fig. 5-65

Fig. 5-66

Fig. 5-67

6. Turn 1/4″ under. Pin in place. Topstitch (Fig. 5-68).

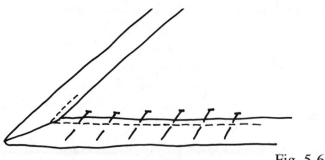

Fig. 5-68

Binding Curved or Shaped Edges

(This method is very popular for straight edges, too.)

1. Trim backing and batting even with quilt top.

2. Cut bias strips 2-1/4″ wide. Sew end to end (Fig. 5-69).

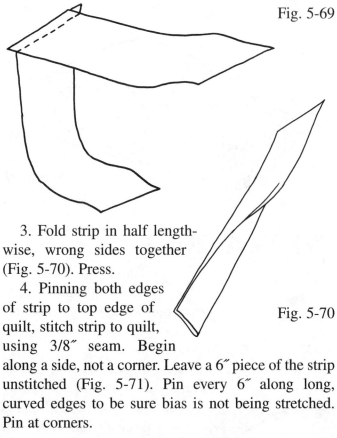

Fig. 5-69

Fig. 5-70

3. Fold strip in half lengthwise, wrong sides together (Fig. 5-70). Press.

4. Pinning both edges of strip to top edge of quilt, stitch strip to quilt, using 3/8″ seam. Begin along a side, not a corner. Leave a 6″ piece of the strip unstitched (Fig. 5-71). Pin every 6″ along long, curved edges to be sure bias is not being stretched. Pin at corners.

Folded edge

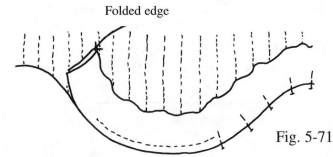

Fig. 5-71

Inside corners. Stitch 3/8″ into corner, lift presser foot to pivot, continue (Fig. 5-72). When bias is turned to back, make a tiny fold with the excess (Fig. 5-73).

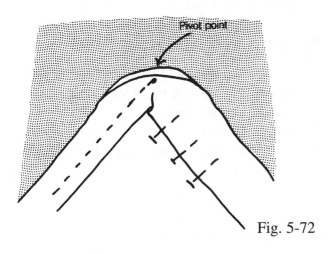

Fig. 5-72

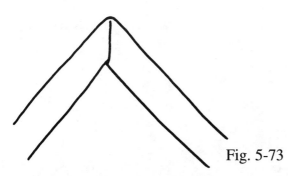

Fig. 5-73

Outside corners. Stop stitching 3/8″ before corner, backtack 1-2 stitches, cut threads. Lift presser foot and fold bias strip as shown (Fig. 5-74). Fold should be even with raw edge. Begin stitching again at fold (Fig. 5-75). When turned to the back, bias will form a neatly mitered corner.

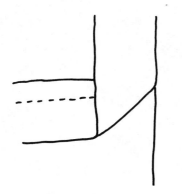

Fig. 5-74

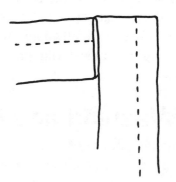

Fig. 5-75

Turn bias to back of quilt. Hand-stitch folded edge to quilt, covering machine stitching. Use same stitch as for hand appliqué.

Innovative Edges

There are several books available with interesting treatments for the edges of quilts. Two of my favorite techniques for curved and shaped edges are:

1. Appliquéing the edge to a straight border. Just cut borders wide enough to go under the innermost dip in the quilt's edge. Pin and appliqué.

2. Applying a facing. I've done this to the Grandmother's Flower Garden shown in this book (see the color section). I like to preserve the hexagon shapes because I think it's an interesting edge. But binding that particular quilt is (to me) a hateful, masochistic process! So I simply reproduce the entire outer ring of hexagons and stitch them, right sides together along the outer edge of the quilt. Turn this to the back, press, and appliqué in place.

CARING FOR YOUR QUILT

When making a quilt that will someday be washed, be sure to preshrink the fabric that is used to make it. At the same time, check fabrics to be sure they won't bleed when wet. (See Preparing Your Fabric for Quilting, page 28.)

Machine Washing and Drying

Machine washing and drying work fine provided you have used a bonded batting and have a washer and dryer large enough to accommodate your quilt.

Use the gentlest cycle and a mild detergent. Use your dryer on the delicate cycle only. **Never** use a hot dryer. Dry only to a slightly damp stage. Remove quilt and finish the drying process flat on a blanket or bed.

Hand Washing and Drying

Fill the bathtub half full of lukewarm water. Use a mild detergent. Squeeze gently and swish the quilt around in the water, but never lift it while it is wet. The weight of the wet quilt at the bottom will snap the quilting threads. Rinse several times. Squeeze as much moisture from the quilt as possible. **Do not wring or lift**. When transporting a wet quilt, fold it into a bundle and carry it in your arms. Dry your quilt on a blanket spread out on a large, flat surface, such as the floor in a spare bedroom. Drying it outside on a sunny day works well, but be sure to put the top side down to prevent fading.

Storage

Fold your quilt loosely and wrap it in a sheet or pillowcase. Never store it in plastic. Air must circulate around the quilt to preserve it. An old custom was to spread the quilts in layers across a bed in an unused room, rotating them so the one on top was constantly changing.

They're finished! Let's show them off! Front (l. to r.): Connie Tzu-Hsun Wu, Brenda Place, Dotti Reynolds, Donna Poster; back (l. to r.): Barbara Johnson, Josephine Rainwater, JoAnn Long, Susan Gradick, Linda Crabtree, and Sarah Francis.

Nine-Patch Chain. Maroon and white, 83" x 101". Machine-pieced and machine-quilted by Josephine Rainwater.

Windmill. Green and red prints, 64" x 84". Machine-stitched and machine-quilted by Donna Poster.

Grandmother's Flower Garden. Teal, yellow, and multicolored solids and florals, 66" x 89". Hand-pieced by Donna Poster and hand-quilted by Sarah Francis.

Texas Trellis. Purple, green, gold, and cream, 56" x 80". Machine-pieced and machine-quilted by Barbara Johnson.

Texas Trellis. Greens and black, 58" x 58". Machine-stitched and machine-quilted by Donna Poster.

Fan. Black, brown, rust, wine, gray, and beige, 50" x 60". Machine-pieced and hand-appliquéd by Linda Crabtree and machine-quilted by The Quilting Loft.

Dresden Plate. Multicolored blacks, brick red, and beige, 60" x 72". Machine-pieced, machine-appliquéd, and machine-quilted by Donna Poster.

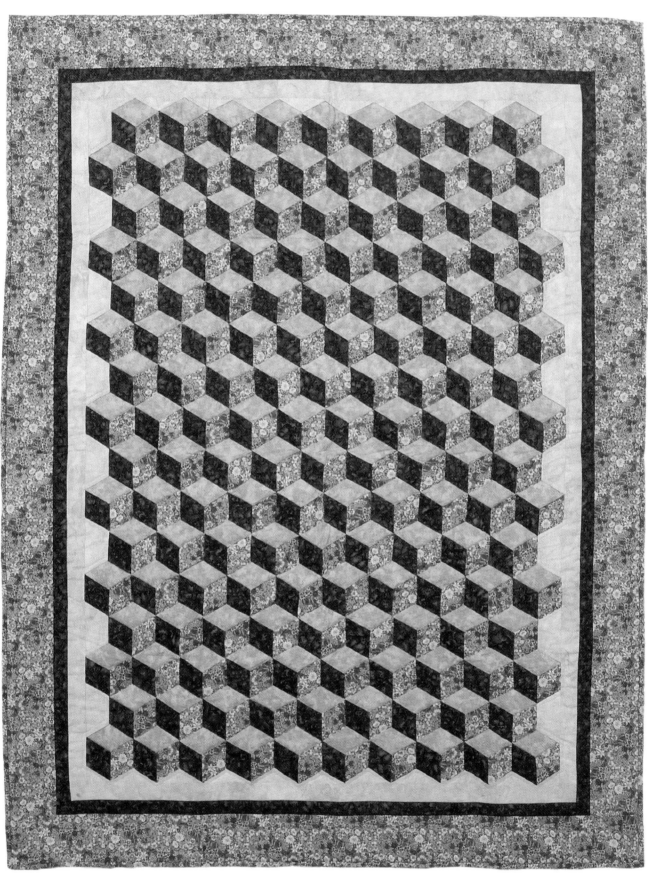

Tumbling Blocks. Pink, yellow, green, and floral, 42" x 56". Machine-stitched by Dottie Reynolds and machine-quilted by The Quilting Loft.

Bow Tie. Black, gray, white, and wine, 60" x 72". Machine-pieced by Connie Tzu-Hsun Wu and machine-quilted by The Quilting Loft.

Floating Stars. Blue and yellow, 58" x 72". Machine-pieced and machine-quilted by Brenda Place.

Piney Woods. Greens, browns, and beiges, 40" x 57". Machine-pieced and machine-quilted by Donna Poster.

Always Friends, a Charm Quilt. Multicolored prints, 55" x 66". Hand-pieced and hand-quilted by Donna Poster.

Magnolias. Green, purple, floral, and light yellow, 88" x 110". Machine-pieced by Dottie Reynolds and machine-quilted by The Quilting Loft.

Clamshell. Multicolored prints, with black and pink borders, 56" x 73". Machine-appliquéd and machine-quilted by Donna Poster.

Love Ring. Lavender, green, and cream, 60" x 76" (4" squares). Machine-pieced by Susan Gradick and machine-quilted by The Quilting Loft.

Love Ring. Salmon, pink, lavender, and blue on light floral, 49" x 60". Machine-pieced and machine-quilted by Donna Poster.

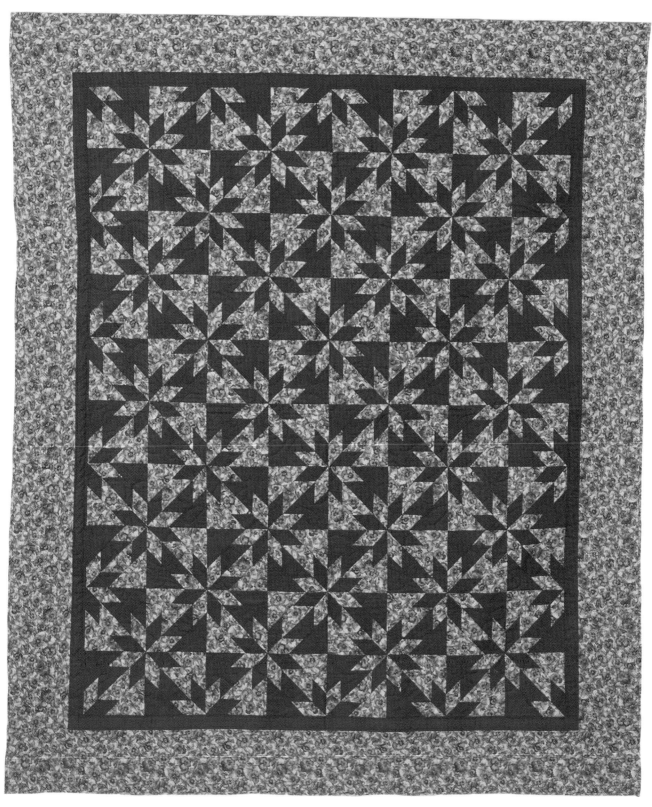

Indian Star. Maroon and green, 60" x 72". Machine-pieced by JoAnn Long and machine-quilted by The Quilting Loft.

Aunt Sukey's Choice. Purple, orange, and gold, 58" x 72". Machine-pieced and machine-quilted by Donna Poster.

Six-Point Star. Multicolored and beige "marbles," 84" x 102". Machine-pieced by Donna Poster and machine-quilted by The Quilting Loft.

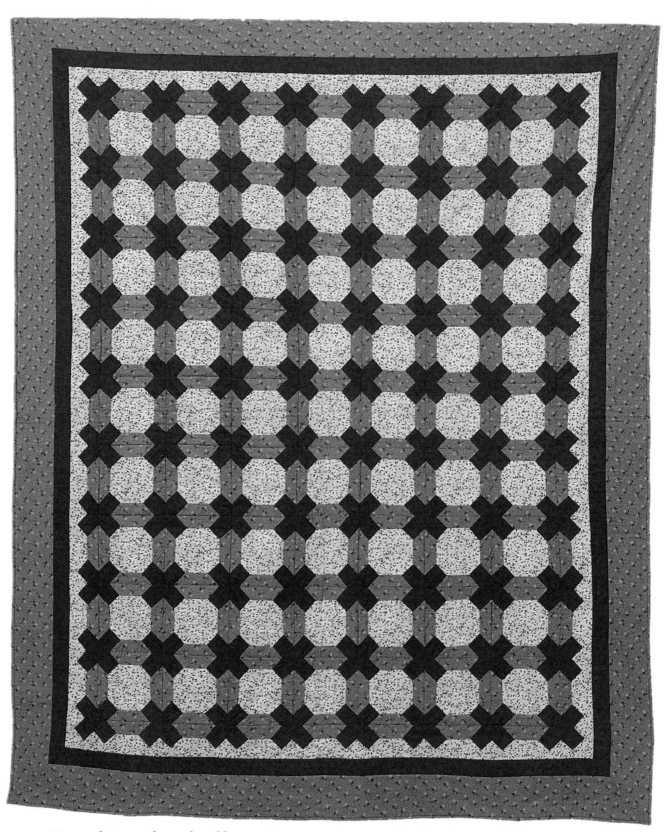

Hugs and Kisses. Blue, red, and beige, 60" x 72". Machine-pieced and machine-quilted by Janet Warner.

Hugs and Kisses. Black, gray, and red, 47" x 60". Machine-pieced and machine-quilted by Donna Poster.

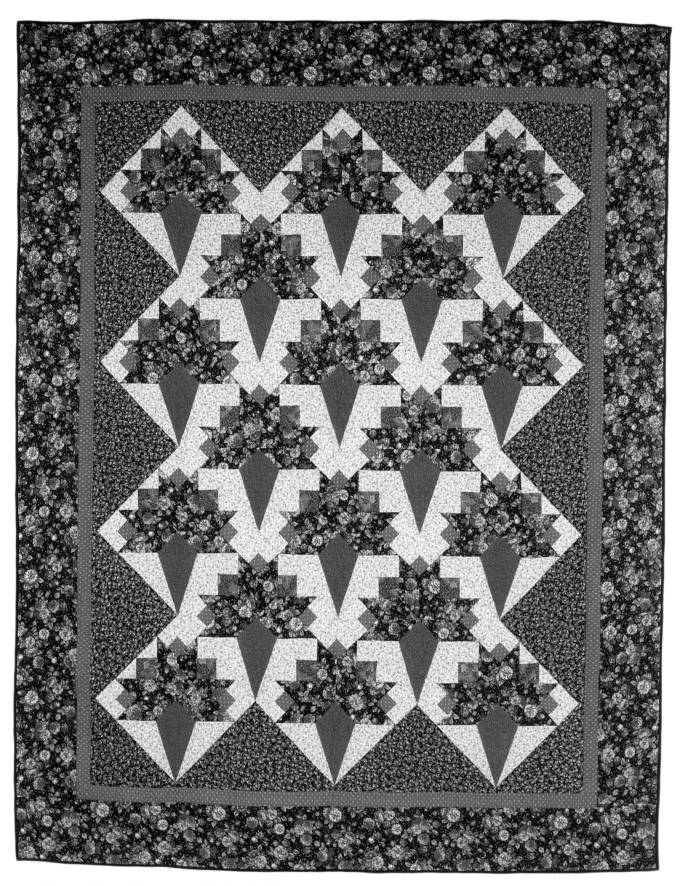

Nosegay. Navy, pink, green, and white floral, 68" x 85". Machine-pieced by Donna Poster and machine-quilted by The Quilting Loft.

Double Wedding Ring. Brown, pink, and beige, 63" x 74". Machine-pieced and machine-quilted by Donna Poster.

Double Wedding Ring. Blue-greens and cream, 41" x 53". Machine-pieced and machine-quilted by Donna Poster.

6 20 QUILTS

Now for the fun part: Making a real quilt!

I assume you've practiced my Speedy System enough to understand the basic principles. Well, good—you need to do that. But learning to quilt is really like learning to play the piano. Practicing the scales is necessary, but the real fun comes when you get to play the songs.

So, as a kind of bonus, I've included 20 quilts to get you going. Some are old favorites, and some are new, but they've all been tested in my classes and they're all fun!

A few explanations about this quilt section:

1. The abbreviations are CR (crib), TW (twin), D (double), Q (queen), K (king), SQ (square), and OB (oblong).

2. The bedspread sizes (TW-K) include a 12-14˝ drop to cover the top of a dust ruffle. They are all long enough to go over a pillow and tuck under it. The square and oblong sizes make nice tablecloths, wall hangings, lap throws, or children's blankets.

3. Each quilt includes a design page to be used as a quick reference or design-your-own. Copy the page, trim the copy to the desired size, and color your design.

4. **For quilts with borders:** To cut the length of the outer borders, add 6˝ to the finished size of the quilt. Cut all other borders to the finished quilt size and trim as needed. All outer borders include 1-1/2˝ extra to turn back for a finished edge.

5. **Yardage notes:** Yardages for all quilts include a small amount for shrinkage and waste. **For quilts with borders:** The yardages are for pieced borders to conserve fabric. You may prefer an unpieced border, especially on wider borders. Use the longest side of your finished quilt to determine how many yards to purchase

6. For clarity, I have tried to keep my instructions simple. If you need further help on any sewing technique, look in Chapter 5, Basic Construction Techniques.

I've divided the quilts into four categories:

1. NINE-PATCH CHAIN
BEGINNER: SUPER EASY

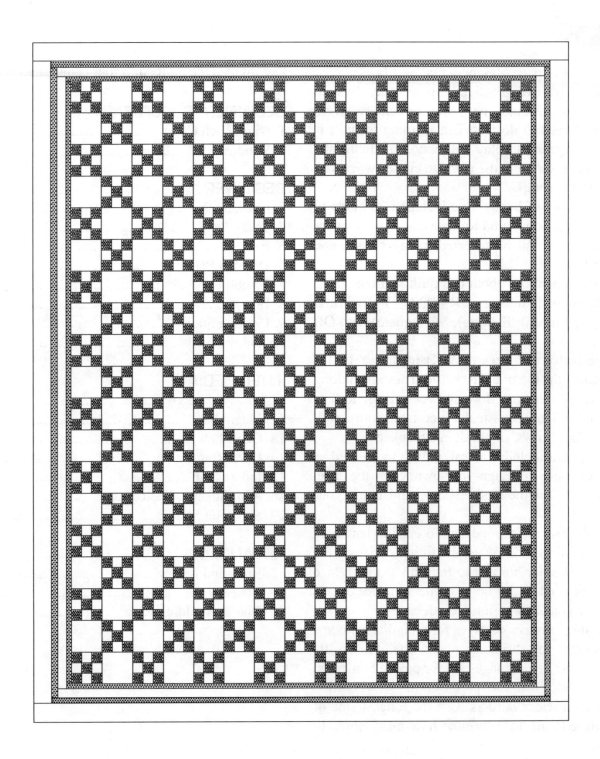

To Speed-Cut:

See Cutting Basic Strips, page 17.

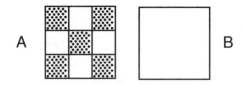

Cutting and Piecing Blocks

A. Block A:

Step 1. Cut strips 2″ wide.

Step 2. Stitch strips together in sets (Fig. 1). Press seams toward the dark fabric (width of sets should measure 5″). (For information on pressing, see Chapter 5.)

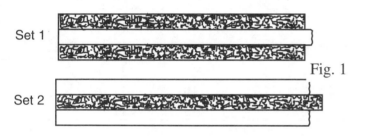

Fig. 1

Step 3. Cut 2″ wide strips from sets (Fig. 2).

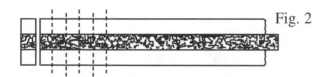

Fig. 2

Step 4. Sew strips together to make Block A (Fig. 3).

Block A   Set 1 / Set 2 / Set 1

Fig. 3

B. Block B:

Step 1. Cut strips 5″ wide.

Step 2. Cut pieces 5″ wide from strips to make Block B (Fig. 4).

Block B

Fig. 4

C. Sewing the Blocks together:

Step 1. Sew blocks in strips (Fig. 5). Press seams toward **unpieced** blocks.

Step 2. Sew strips together (Fig. 6). Press all seams in the same direction.

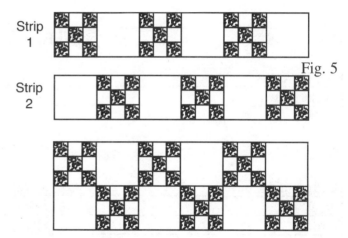

Fig. 5

Fig. 6

D. Add borders. (See page 41)

Finishing

A. Quilt as desired.

B. Bind edges. (For information on binding, see Binding the Edges, page 45.)

DIMENSIONS (INCHES)

	CR	TW	D	Q	K	SQ	OB
Finished Quilt	51x60	72x99	83x101	88x106	108x108	64x64	61x70
Center	41x50	50x77	59x77	68x86	86x86	50x50	50x59
Border 1	1-1/2	1-1/2	1-1/2	1-1/2	1-1/2	1-1/2	1-1/2
Border 2	3-1/2	2-1/2	2-1/2	2-1/2	2-1/2	5-1/2	4
Border 3	-	7	8	6	7	-	-

CUTTING INSTRUCTIONS

	CR	TW	D	Q	K	SQ	OB
Chain Strips							
2″ wide	13	25	30	38	48	18	20
Background Strips							
2″ wide	11	20	24	31	39	15	16
Background Strips							
5″ wide	7	12	14	18	23	8	9
Border 1	2″	2″	2″	2″	2″	2″	2″
Border 2	5″	3″	3″	3″	3″	7″	5-1/2″
Border 3	-	8-1/2″	9-1/2″	7-1/2″	8-1/2″	-	-

For additional information on cutting borders, see page 73.

Sets Needed

	CR	TW	D	Q	K	SQ	OB
Set 1	5	10	12	15	19	7	8
Set 2	3	5	6	8	10	4	4
Blocks needed							
A (pieced)	50	94	111	143	181	61	72
B (unpieced)	49	93	110	142	180	60	71

GENERAL INFORMATION

	CR	TW	D	Q	K	SQ	OB
Blocks Across	9	11	13	15	19	11	11
Blocks Down	11	17	17	19	19	11	13

YARDAGES

	CR	TW	D	Q	K	SQ	OB
Background	2	3-1/2	3-3/4	4-3/4	6	2-1/4	2-1/2
Chain	1	1-3/4	2	2-1/2	3	1-1/4	1-1/2
Border 1	1/2	1/2	3/4	3/4	7/8	1/2	1/2
Border 2	3/4	1	1-1/8	1	1	1-1/2	1-1/8
Border 3	-	2-1/8	2-1/2	2	2-5/8	-	-
Backing	3-1/4	6-3/4	8-1/2	8-1/2	10-3/4	4	3-3/4

For additional information on yardages, see page 73.

OPTIONS

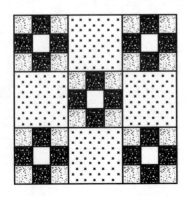 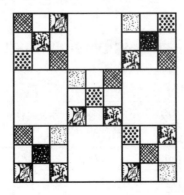 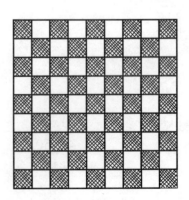

NINE-PATCH CHAIN
DESIGN PAGE

For a quick reference or design-your-own:
1. Copy this page.
2. Trim copy to desired quilt size.
3. Color design.

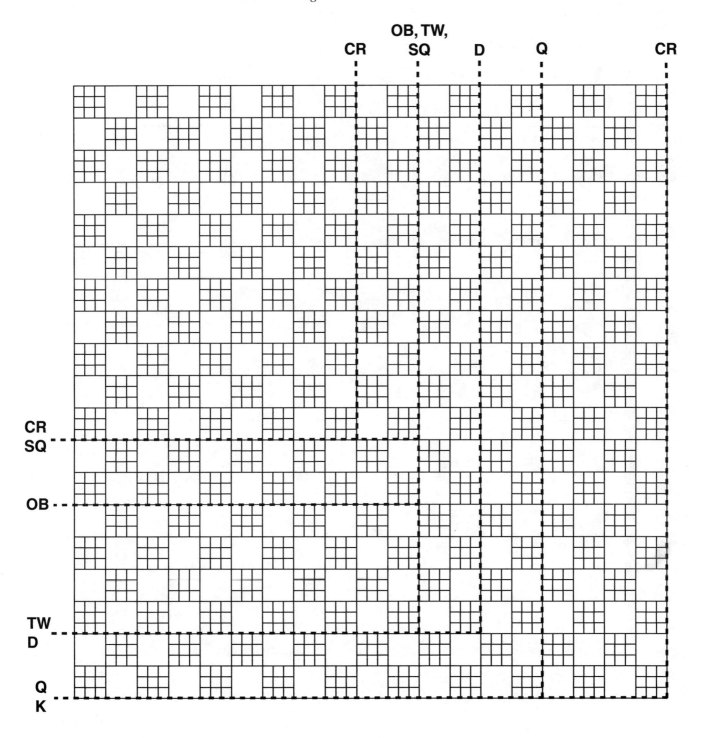

2. WINDMILL
BEGINNER: SUPER EASY

INSTRUCTIONS

To Speed-Cut:

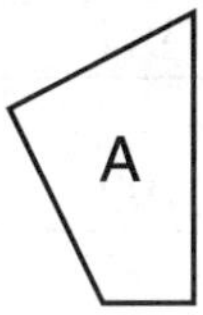

A. Cone, Two 90° Angles (see B, Cutting Notes)

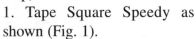

B. Cutting Notes: (Stack all fabric right side up)

1. Tape Square Speedy as shown (Fig. 1).
2. Cut rectangles 3-1/8″ x 7-1/2″. From these cut A pieces (Fig. 2).

Fig. 1

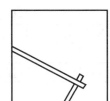

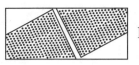

Fig. 2

Piecing

A. Piecing basic blocks:

Step 1. Piece units as shown (Fig 3).

Step 2. Join units into squares (Fig. 4).

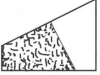

Step 3. Join squares to make blocks (Fig. 5).

Fig. 3

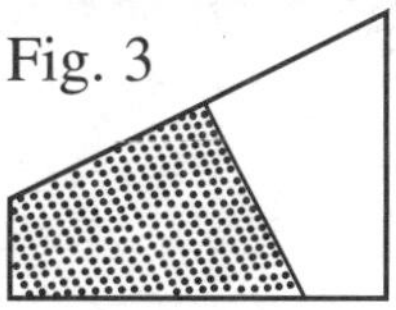

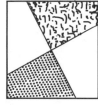

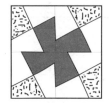

Fig. 4

Fig. 5

B. Joining blocks:

Step 1. Join blocks to form rows (Fig. 6).

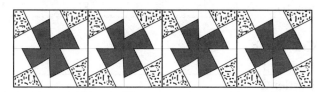

Fig. 6

Step 2. Join rows (Fig. 7).

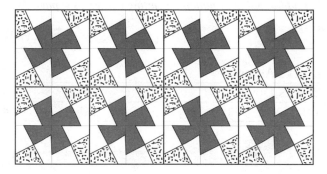

Fig. 7

C. Add borders. (See page 41)

Finishing

A. Quilt as desired.

B. Bind edges. (For information on binding, see Binding the Edges, page 45.)

DIMENSIONS (INCHES)

	CR	TW	D	Q	K	SQ	OB
Finished Quilt	50x60	72x102	84x104	88x108	104x104	64x64	54x74
Center	40x50	50x80	60x80	60x80	80x80	50x50	40x60
Border 1	1-1/2	1-1/2	1-1/2	2	2	2	2
Border 2	3-1/2	3	3	4	4	5	5
Border 3	-	1-1/2	1-1/2	2	6	-	-
Border 4	-	5	6	6	-	-	-

CUTTING INSTRUCTIONS

	CR	TW	D	Q	K	SQ	OB
A - Background	160	320	384	384	512	200	192
A - Fabric 1 & 2 (each)	80	160	192	192	256	100	96
Cut Width							
Border 1	2″	2″	2″	2-1/2″	2-1/2″	2-1/2″	2-1/2″
Border 2	5″	3-1/2″	3-1/2″	4-1/2″	4-1/2″	6-1/2″	6-1/2″
Border 3	-	2″	2″	2-1/2″	7-1/2″	-	-
Border 4	-	6-1/2″	7-1/2″	7-1/2″	-	-	-

For additional information on cutting borders, see page 73.

GENERAL INFORMATION

	CR	TW	D	Q	K	SQ	OB
Blocks Across	4	5	6	6	8	5	4
Blocks Down	5	8	8	8	8	5	6
Total	20	40	48	48	64	25	24

YARDAGES

	CR	TW	D	Q	K	SQ	OB
Background	1-3/4	3-1/4	3-3/4	3-3/4	5	2	2
Fabric 1 & 2 (each)	1	1-3/4	2	2	3	1	1
Border 1	1/2	3/4	3/4	1	1	3/4	3/4
Border 2	1-1/4	1	1-1/4	1-1/2	1-3/4	1-3/4	1-1/2
Border 3	-	3/4	3/4	1	3	-	-
Border 4	-	2	2-1/2	2-1/2	-	-	-
Backing	3-1/4	6-3/4	8-1/2	8-1/2	10-1/4	4	3-3/4

For additional information on yardages, see page 73.

OPTIONS

  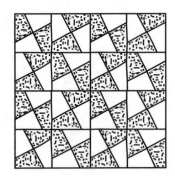

FULL-SIZE TEMPLATE

Templates include a 1/4" seam allowance

WINDMILL
DESIGN PAGE

For a quick reference or design-your-own:
1. Copy this page.
2. Trim copy to desired quilt size.
3. Color design.

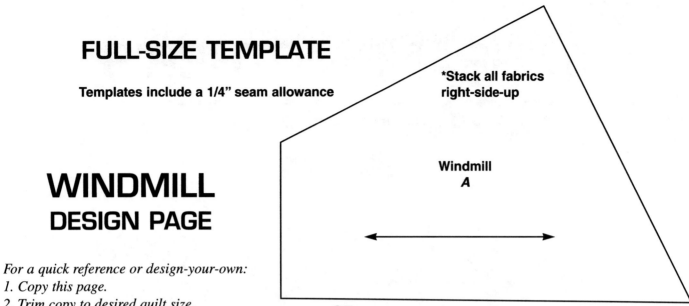

*Stack all fabrics right-side-up

Windmill
A

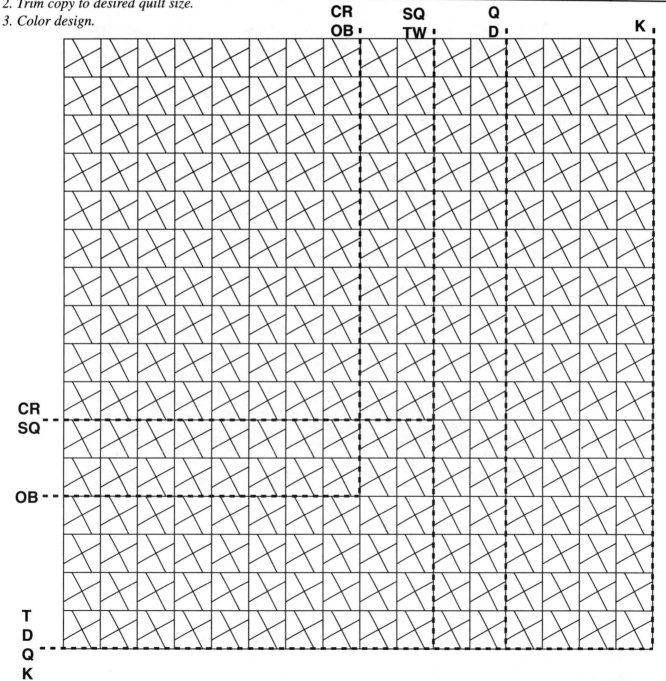

CR OB

SQ TW

Q D

K

CR SQ

OB

T D Q K

3. GRANDMOTHER'S FLOWER GARDEN
BEGINNER

INSTRUCTIONS

To Speed-Cut:

A. Hexagon

NOTE: This is one of the few quilts that actually takes longer to machine-piece than to hand-piece. Believe me—I've tried it! Try my method for hand-piecing with no marked seam lines (See Chapter 5)—it's easy and fun.

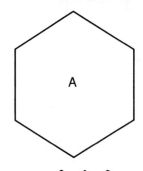

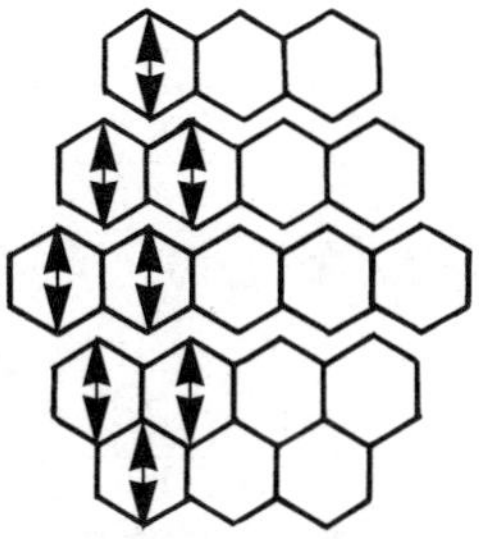

Fig. 1

Piecing

A. Piecing basic units:

Step 1. Join flower pieces in rows (Fig. 1).

NOTE: Pieces will fit better if grain in all pieces are in the same direction.

Step 2. Join these rows (Fig. 2).

Fig. 2

B. Joining units:

Step 1. Sew two connecting pieces between flower units (Fig. 3).

Fig. 3

Step 2. Join connecting pieces to form horizontal rows (Fig. 4).

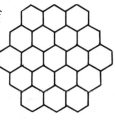

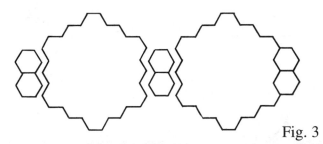

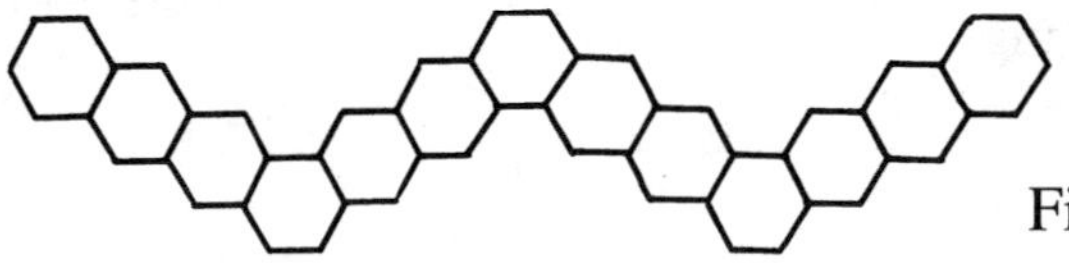

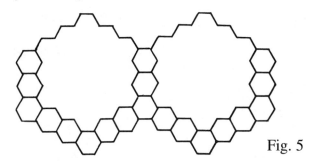

Fig. 4

Step 3. Join flower rows and connecting rows (Fig. 5).

Fig. 5

Finishing

A. Quilt as desired.

B. Cut bias binding 2-1/4″ wide. Bind, following "stepped" edges.

DIMENSIONS (INCHES)

	CR	TW	D	Q	K	SQ	OB
Finished Quilt	34x50	67x103	80x103	93x103	106x103	43x50	43x68

CUTTING INSTRUCTIONS

	CR	TW	D	Q	K	SQ	OB
Number Needed							
Centers (Fabric 1)	17	49	58	67	76	22	31
1st Ring (Fabric 2)	94	278	332	386	440	120	174
2nd Ring (Fabric 3)	184	548	656	764	872	244	342
Connectors (Fabric 4)	150	410	488	566	644	196	264
Binding	Cut bias strips 2-1/4″ wide						

GENERAL INFORMATION

	CR	TW	D	Q	K	SQ	OB
Rings Across	3	5	6	7	8	4	4
Rings Down	5	9	9	9	9	5	7
Total	13	41	50	59	68	18	25
Total Half-rings	4	8	8	8	8	6	6

YARDAGES

	CR	TW	D	Q	K	SQ	OB
Fabric 1 - (centers)	1/4	1/2	5/8	3/4	3/4	1/4	3/8
Fabric 2 - (1st ring)	3/4	2-1/4	2-7/8	3-1/4	3-5/8	1	1-1/4
Fabric 3 - (2nd ring)	1-1/4	4-1/2	5-1/2	6-1/4	7-1/8	1-1/2	2-1/4
Fabric 4 - (connecting rings)	1	3-1/2	4	4-1/2	5-1/4	1-3/8	1-3/4
Backing	1-3/4	6	6	8-1/4	9-1/4	2-3/4	2-3/4
Binding	1/2	1-1/4	1-1/2	1-1/2	1-3/4	1/2	3/4

For additional information on yardages, see page 73.

OPTIONS

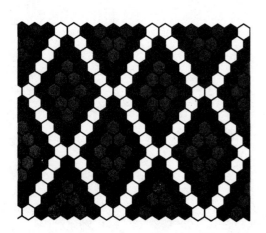

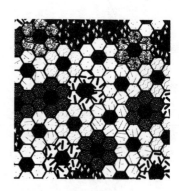

FULL-SIZE TEMPLATE

Templates include a 1/4" seam allowance

GRANDMOTHER'S
FLOWER GARDEN
DESIGN PAGE

For a quick reference or design-your-own:
1. Copy this page.
2. Trim copy to desired quilt size.
3. Color design.

C-TW-SQ-OB

D-Q-K

**Grandmother's
Flower Garden
A**

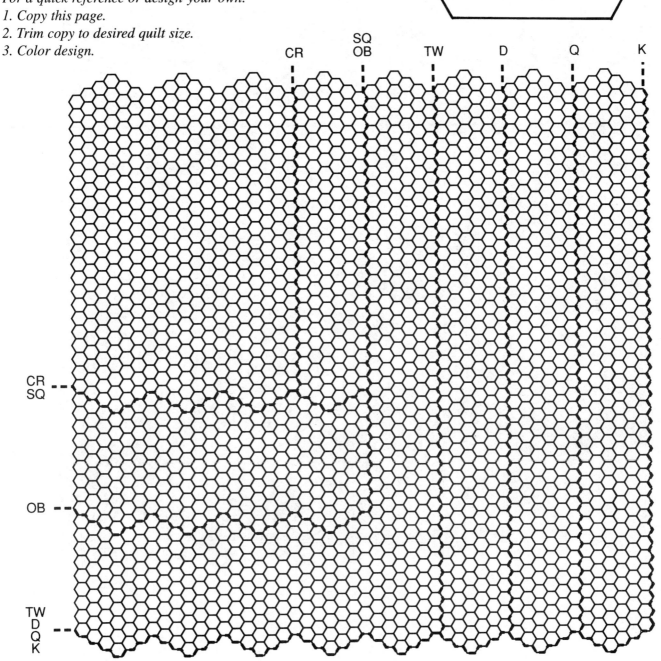

4. TEXAS TRELLIS
BEGINNER

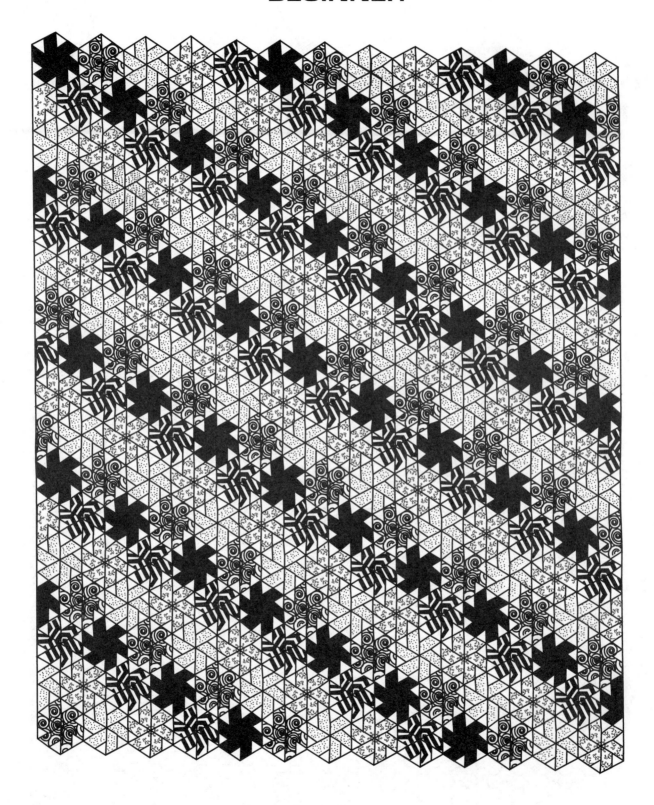

To Speed-Cut:
  A. Wedge, 60°
  B. Wedge, 60°

Cutting Note: If speed-cutting, all strips must be cut on the lengthwise grain. Cut all basic strips 2-1/4″ wide. (Cutting the tip from B allows all strips to be cut the same width, reducing error.)

Piecing
A. Piecing basic units:

Step 1. Join A and B pieces as shown (Fig. 1). (Joining tipless "point" on this seam places straight edge of B to best advantage.) (Fig. 2).

Step 2. Join units to form half hexagons. Stitch together in order shown. Press as

Fig. 1

Fig. 2

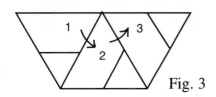

Fig. 3

arrows indicate (Fig. 3).

B. Joining units:

Step 1. Join units to form strips (Fig. 4).

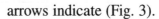

Fig. 4

Step 2. Join strips (Fig. 5).

Fig. 5

Finishing
A. Quilt as desired.
B. Cut bias binding 2-1/4″ wide. Bind, following "stepped" edges.

DIMENSIONS (INCHES)

	CR	TW	D	Q	K	SQ	OB
Finished Size	42x56	70x104	84x104	91x104	105x104	35x38	56x80

CUTTING INSTRUCTIONS

	CR	TW	D	Q	K	SQ	OB
Number Needed A - Fabrics 1-5 (each)	66	204	246	270	306	42	126
B - Fabric 6 (background)	324	1020	1224	1326	1530	210	624
Binding	Cut bias strips 2-1/4″ wide						

GENERAL INFORMATION

	CR	TW	D	Q	K	SQ	OB
Number of units Across	6	10	12	13	15	5	8
Number of units Down (rows)	9	17	17	17	17	7	13
Total	54	170	204	221	255	35	104

YARDAGES

	CR	TW	D	Q	K	SQ	OB
Fabrics 1-5 (each)	3/4	1-3/4	2	2-1/4	2-1/2	3/8	1
Fabric 6 (background)	1-1/4	3-1/2	4-1/4	4-1/2	5-1/4	3/4	2-1/4
Backing	3	6-1/2	7-3/4	8-1/2	10-1/4	1-1/8	3-3/4
Binding	3/4	1-1/4	1-1/2	1-1/2	1-3/4	1/2	1

For additional information on yardages, see page 73.

OPTIONS

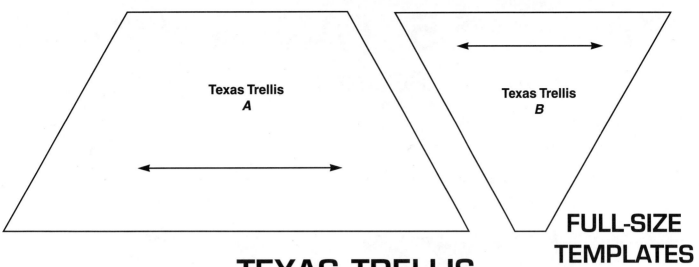

Texas Trellis
A

Texas Trellis
B

TEXAS TRELLIS
DESIGN PAGE

FULL-SIZE TEMPLATES

**Templates include a 1/4"
seam allowance**

For a quick reference or design-your-own:
1. Copy this page.
2. Trim copy to desired quilt size.
3. Color design.

CR   OB   TW
                    SQ   D   Q   K

CR

SQ

OB

TW-D
Q-K

5. FAN
BEGINNER

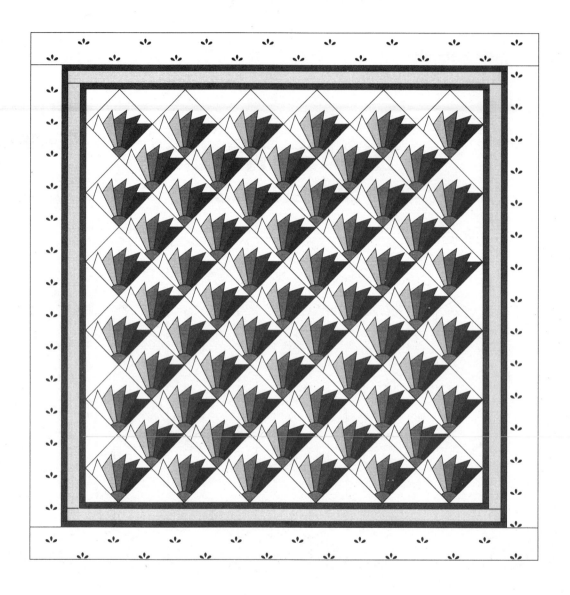

To Speed-Cut:

A. Cone, Point End

B. Fan

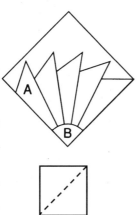

Background Blocks: cut 10-1/2″ x 10-1/2″

Squares for Edge Triangles: Cut 12″ x 12″ (cut in half diagonally) (See pages 40-41)

Squares for Corner Triangles: Cut 9″ x 9″ (cut in half diagonally)

Cutting Note: All fabrics used for A must be stacked right side up.

Piecing

A. Piecing blocks:

Step 1. Press outer edge of cone 1/4″ to wrong side (Fig. 1).

Step 2. Join cones, stitching across pressed end of cones (Fig. 2).

Step 3. Press seams toward long side, pressing under unstitched edge also. Trim corner (Fig. 3).

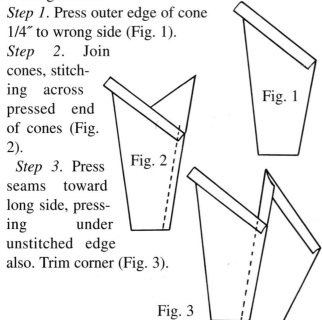

Fig. 1

Fig. 2

Fig. 3

Step 4. Pin fan to block.

Step 5. With running stitch and pressing template, prepare piece B for appliqué (Fig. 4). Pin on corner of fan (Fig. 5).

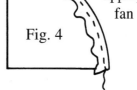

Fig. 4

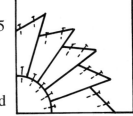

Fig. 5

Step 6. Machine or hand appliqué pinned edges.

B. Joining blocks and triangles:

Fig.6

Step 1. Join units to form strips (Fig. 6).

Step 2. Join strips. (See Sewing the Quilts Blocks Together and On-Point Blocks, pages 40-41.)

C. Add borders.

Finishing

A. Quilt as desired.

B. Bind edges.

DIMENSIONS (INCHES)

	CR	TW	D	Q	K	SQ	OB
Finished Quilt	46x64	76x104	90x104	92x106	110x110	66x66	59x73
Center	40x58	58x86	72x86	72x86	86x86	58x58	43x57
Border 1	3	1-1/2	1-1/2	1-1/2	1-1/2	1	1-1/2
Border 2	-	3	3	3	3	3	2-1/2
Border 3	-	4-1/2	4-1/2	5-1/2	1-1/2	-	4
Border 4	-	-	-	-	6	-	-

CUTTING INSTRUCTIONS

	CR	TW	D	Q	K	SQ	OB
Number Needed							
A - Fabric 1-5							
(each)	18	39	50	50	61	25	18
B - Fabric 6	18	39	50	50	61	25	18
Background Squares							
Fabric 7	18	39	50	50	61	25	18
Edge Triangles							
Fabric 7	10	16	18	18	20	12	10
Corner Triangles							
Fabric 7	4	4	4	4	4	4	4
Cut Widths							
Border 1	4-1/2″	2″	2″	2″	2″	1-1/2″	2″
Border 2	-	3-1/2″	3-1/2″	3-1/2″	3-1/2″	4-1/2″	3″
Border 3	-	6″	6″	7″	2″	-	5-1/2″
Border 4	-	-	-	-	7-1/2″	-	-

For additional information on cutting borders, see page 73.

GENERAL INFORMATION

	CR	TW	D	Q	K	SQ	OB
Blocks Across	3	4	5	5	6	4	3
Blocks Down	4	6	6	6	6	4	4
Total	18	39	50	50	61	25	18

YARDAGES

	CR	TW	D	Q	K	SQ	OB
A - Fabric 1-5							
(each)	3/8	5/8	7/8	7/8	1	1/2	3/8
B - Fabric 6	1/4	1/2	3/4	3/4	3/4	1/2	1/4
Background Squares							
Fabric 7	2	4-1/4	5-1/4	5-1/4	6-1/2	3	2
Edge & Corner Triangle							
Fabric 7	3/4	1-1/4	1-1/4	1-1/2	1-3/4	1	3/4
Border 1	1-1/4	3/4	3/4	3/4	3/4	1/2	1/2
Border 2	-	1	1-1/4	1-1/4	1-1/2	1-1/4	3/4
Border 3	-	1-3/4	2	2 1/4	3/4	-	1-1/2
Border 4	-	-	-	-	3	-	-
Backing	3-1/4	6-3/4	8-1/2	8-1/2	10-1/4	4	3-3/4

For additional information on yardages, see page 73.

OPTIONS

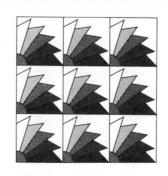
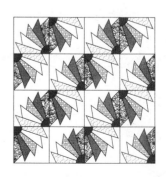

FULL-SIZE TEMPLATES

Background blocks: Cut 10-1/2 x 10-1/2
Squares for edge triangles: Cut 12 x 12 (cut in half diagonally)
Squares for corner triangles: Cut 9 x 9 (cut in half diagonally)

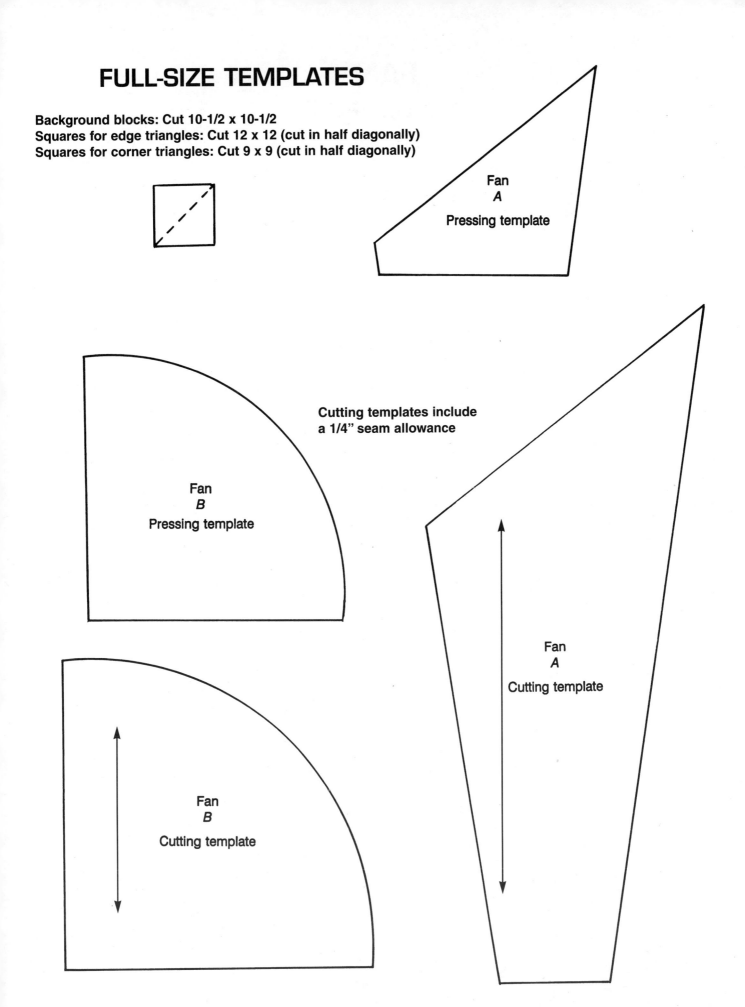

Fan
A
Pressing template

Fan
B
Pressing template

Cutting templates include
a 1/4" seam allowance

Fan
A
Cutting template

Fan
B
Cutting template

FAN
DESIGN PAGE

For a quick reference or design-your-own:
1. Copy this page.
2. Trim copy to desired quilt size.
3. Color design.

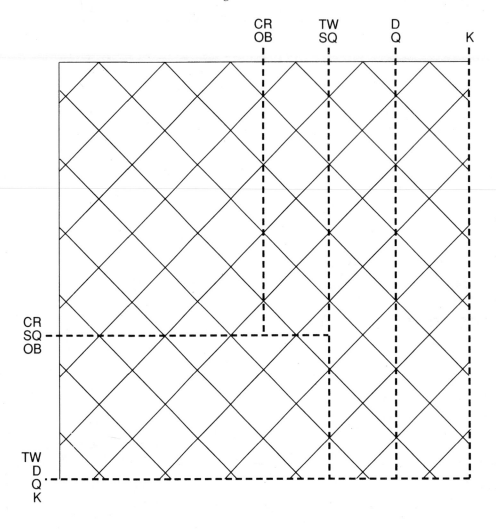

6. DRESDEN PLATE
BEGINNER

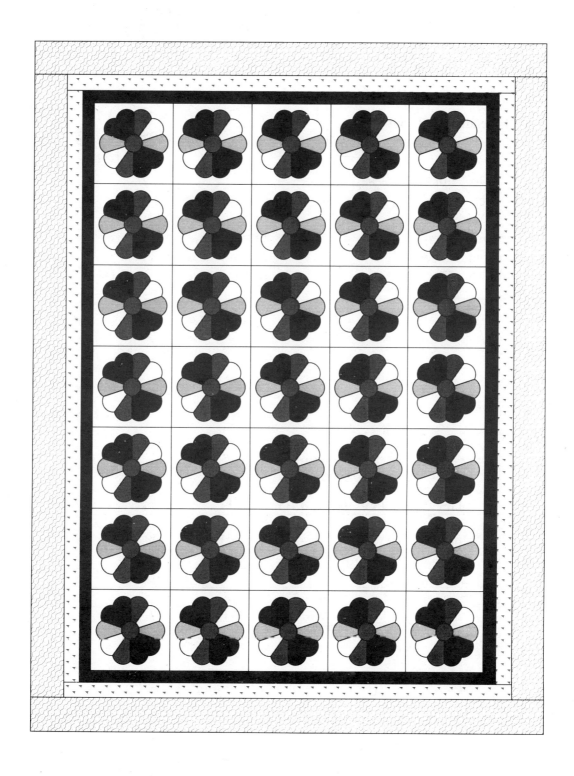

To Speed-Cut:
A. Cone, Arc End
B. Circle, 4˝

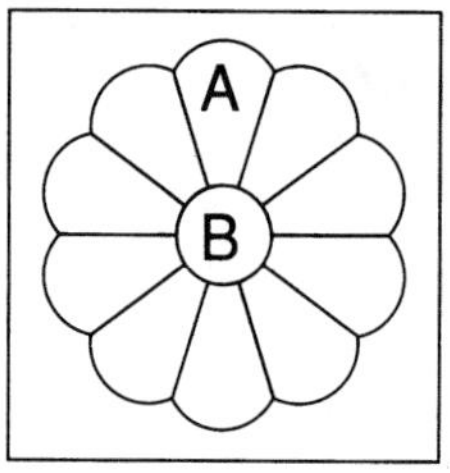

Piecing
A. Piecing blocks:

Step 1. Join cone pieces. Do **not** backstitch (Fig. 1).

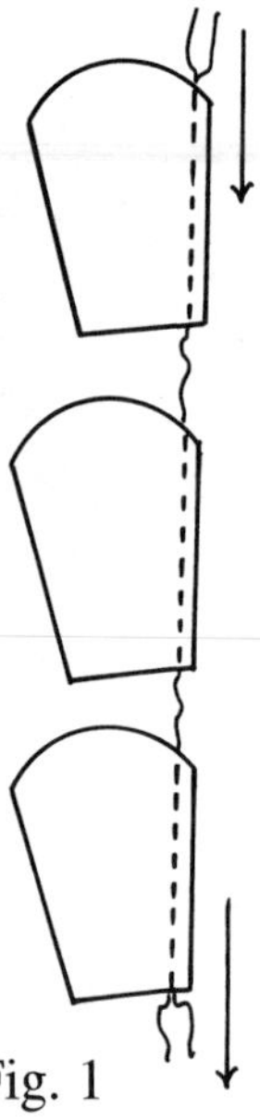

Step 2. Using the eye end of a needle, pull out about 1/2˝ of the seam at the wide end of the cones. Do **not** clip threads (Fig. 2).

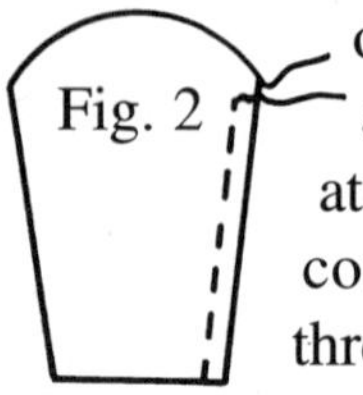

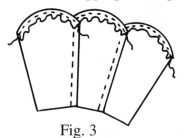

Fig. 2

Step 3. With running stitch and pressing templates, prepare circles and outer edges of cones for appliqué (Fig. 3).

Fig. 3

Fig. 1

NOTE: Seam allowance will be wider than 1/4˝ at ends of arcs (Fig. 4).

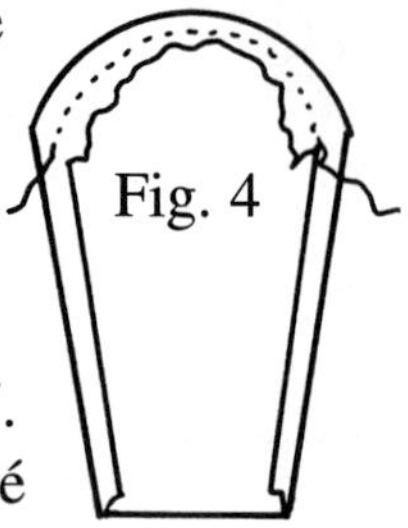

Fig. 4

Step 4. Hand or machine appliqué circles to plates (Fig. 5).

Step 5. Appliqué plates to background squares (Fig.6).

B. Join blocks.
C. Add borders.

Fig. 5

Finishing
A. Quilt as desired.
B. Bind edges.

Fig. 6

DIMENSIONS (INCHES)

	CR	TW	D	Q	K	SQ	OB
Finished Quilt	46x58	70x106	82x106	92x104	108x108	64x64	60x72
Center	36x48	60x96	60x84	72x84	84x84	48x48	48x60
Border 1	1-1/2	1-1/2	1-1/2	1-1/2	1-1/2	1-1/2	1-1/2
Border 2	3-1/2	3-1/2	3	3	3	2-1/2	4-1/2
Border 3	-	-	6-1/2	5-1/2	7-1/2	4	-

CUTTING INSTRUCTIONS

	CR	TW	D	Q	K	SQ	OB
Number Needed							
A - Fabrics 1-5							
(each)	24	80	70	84	98	32	40
B - Fabric 6	12	40	35	42	49	16	20
Background Blocks							
Fabric 7	12	40	35	42	49	16	20
Cut Widths							
Border 1	2″	2″	2″	2″	2″	2″	2″
Border 2	5″	5″	3-1/2″	3-1/2″	3-1/2″	3″	6″
Border 3	-	-	8″	7″	9″	5-1/2″	-

For additional information on cutting borders, see page 73.

GENERAL INFORMATION

	CR	TW	D	Q	K	SQ	OB
Blocks Across	3	5	5	6	7	4	4
Blocks Down	4	8	7	7	7	4	5
Total	12	40	35	42	49	16	20

YARDAGES

	CR	TW	D	Q	K	SQ	OB
A - Fabrics 1-5							
(each)	1/2	1-1/2	1-1/4	1-1/2	1-3/4	3/4	3/4
B - Fabric 6	3/8	3/4	3/4	7/8	7/8	3/8	3/8
Background Blocks							
Fabric 7	1-1/2	5	4-1/2	5	6	2-1/2	2-1/2
Border 1	1/2	3/4	3/4	3/4	3/4	3/4	1/2
Border 2	1-1/4	1-1/2	1-1/4	1-1/4	1-1/2	1	1-1/2
Border 3	-	-	2-1/2	2-1/4	3-1/2	1-1/2	-
Backing	3	6-1/2	8-1/4	8-1/2	10	4	4

For additional information on yardages, see page 73.

OPTIONS

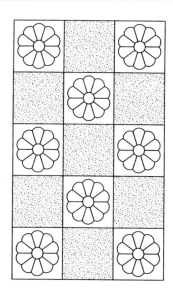 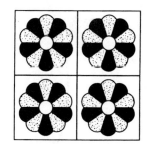 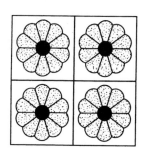

FULL-SIZE TEMPLATES

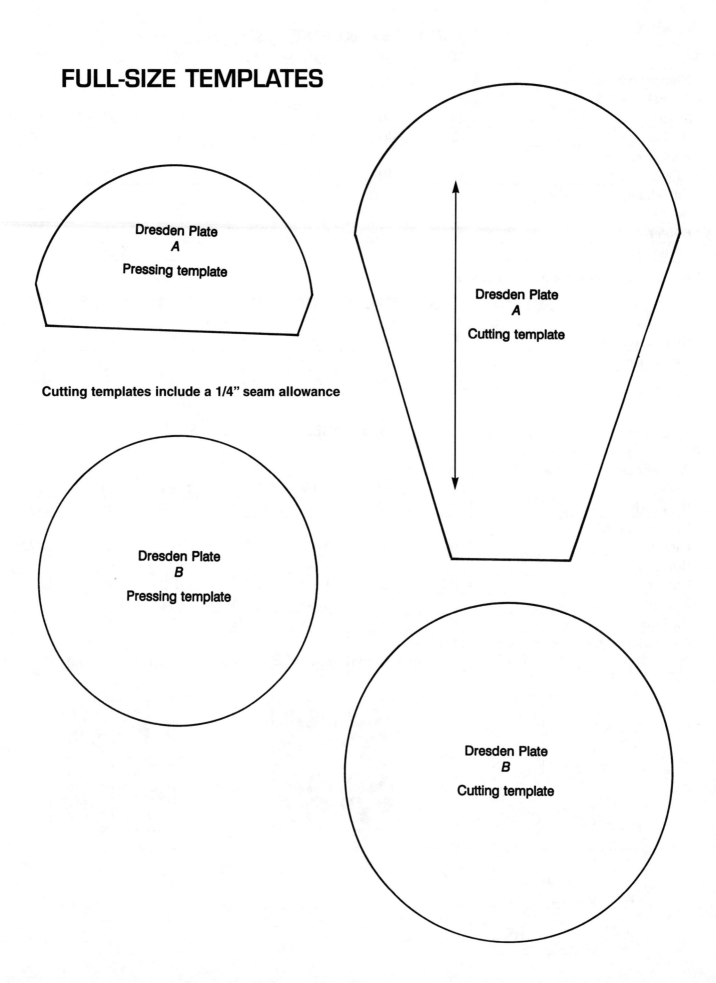

Dresden Plate
A
Pressing template

Cutting templates include a 1/4" seam allowance

Dresden Plate
A
Cutting template

Dresden Plate
B
Pressing template

Dresden Plate
B
Cutting template

DRESDEN PLATE
DESIGN PAGE

For a quick reference or design-your-own:
1. Copy this page.
2. Trim copy to desired quilt size.
3. Color design.

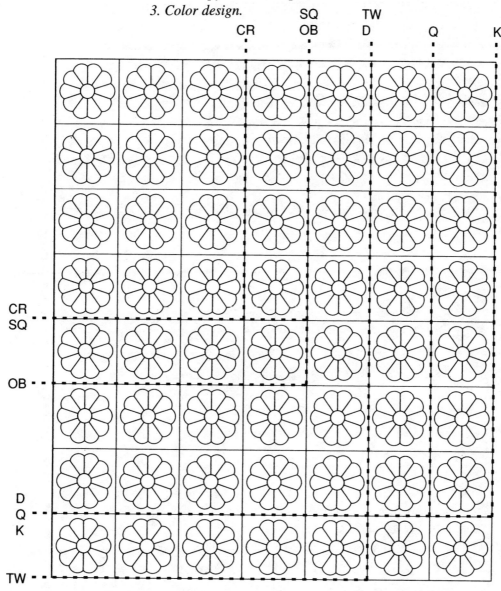

7. TUMBLING BLOCKS
BEGINNER

To Speed-Cut:
A. Diamond, 60°
B. Wedge, 60°
C. Triangle, 60°

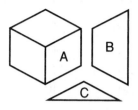

Piecing
NOTE: Two optional piecing methods are presented here. Method 1 is less complicated to follow, but all seams are set-in seams. Method 2 requires more planning, but is faster to sew:

A. Piecing and joining units:

Method 1

Step 1. Piece block units (Fig. 1).

Step 2. Connect blocks to form rows (Fig. 2).

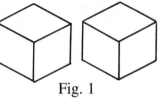

Fig. 1

Fig. 2

Step 3. Join rows (Fig. 3).

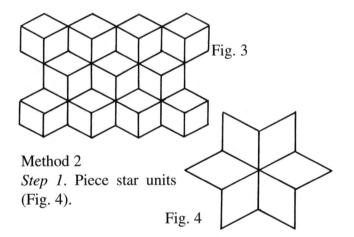

Fig. 3

Method 2

Step 1. Piece star units (Fig. 4).

Fig. 4

Step 2. Add diamonds on three sides (Fig. 5).

Step 3. Join units to form columns (Fig. 6).

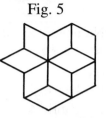

Fig. 5

Fig. 6

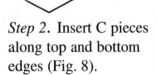

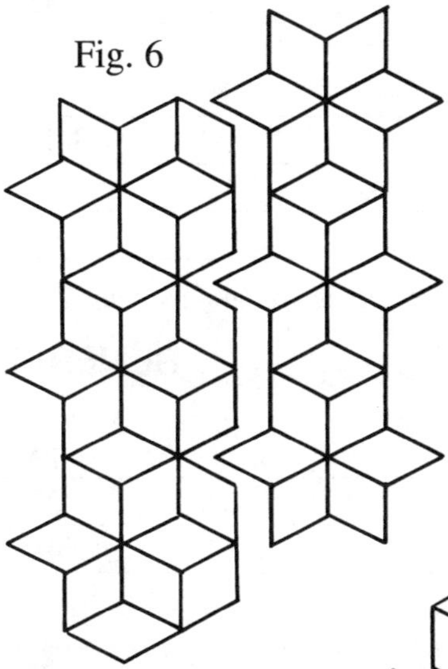

Step 4. Join columns, adding additional diamonds as needed.

B. Adding side edges, both methods:

Step 1. Insert B pieces along both sides (Fig. 7).

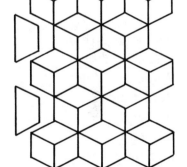

Step 2. Insert C pieces along top and bottom edges (Fig. 8).

Finishing
A. Quilt as desired.
B. Bind edges.

Fig. 7

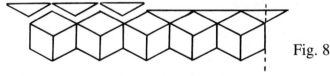

Fig. 8

DIMENSIONS (INCHES)

	CR	TW	D	Q	K	SQ	OB
Finished Quilt	42x56	72x102	83x106	91x106	107x108	66x68	58x76
Center	32x46	52x82	59x82	67x82	81x82	56x58	46x64
Border 1	1-1/2	1-1/2	1-1/2	1-1/2	1-1/2	1-1/2	1-1/2
Border 2	3-1/2	3	3	3	4	3-1/2	4-1/2
Border 3	-	5-1/2	1-1/2	1-1/2	1-1/2	-	-
Border 4	-	-	6	6	6	-	-

CUTTING INSTRUCTIONS

	CR	TW	D	Q	K	SQ	OB
Number Needed							
A - Fabrics 1-3							
(each)	128	392	446	500	608	295	263
B - Fabric 4	14	26	26	26	26	18	20
C - Fabric 4	20	32	36	40	48	34	28
Cut Widths							
Border 1	2″	2″	2″	2″	2″	2″	2″
Border 2	5″	3-1/2″	3-1/2″	3-1/2″	4-1/2″	5″	6″
Border 3	-	7″	2″	2″	2″	-	-
Border 4	-	-	7-1/2″	7-1/2″	7-1/2″	-	-

For additional information on cutting borders, see page 73.

GENERAL INFORMATION

	CR	TW	D	Q	K	SQ	OB
Units Across	9	15	17	19	23	16	13
Units Down (rows)	15	27	27	27	27	19	21
Total	128	392	446	500	608	295	263

YARDAGES

	CR	TW	D	Q	K	SQ	OB
A - Fabric 1 (dark)	7/8	2-1/8	2-1/4	2-5/8	3-1/8	1-3/4	1-1/2
A - Fabric 2 (medium)	7/8	2-1/8	2-1/4	2-5/8	3-1/8	1-3/4	1-1/2
A - Fabric 3 (light)	7/8	2-1/8	2-1/4	2-5/8	3-1/8	1-3/4	1-1/2
B & C - Fabric 4	3/8	1/2	1/2	5/8	5/8	3/8	3/8
Border 1	1/2	1/2	3/4	3/4	3/4	3/4	1/2
Border 2	1-1/4	1	1-1/4	1-1/4	1-3/4	1-1/2	1-1/2
Border 3	-	2	3/4	3/4	3/4	-	-
Border 4	-	-	2-1/2	2-1/2	3	-	-
Backing	3-1/4	6-3/4	8-1/2	8-1/2	10-1/4	4	3-3/4

For additional information on yardages, see page 73.

OPTIONS

FULL-SIZE TEMPLATES

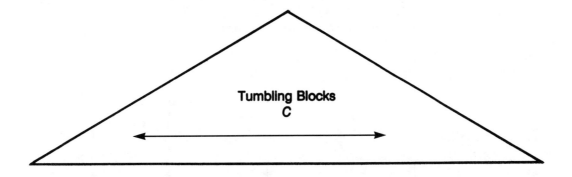

Tumbling Blocks
C

Templates include a 1/4" seam allowance

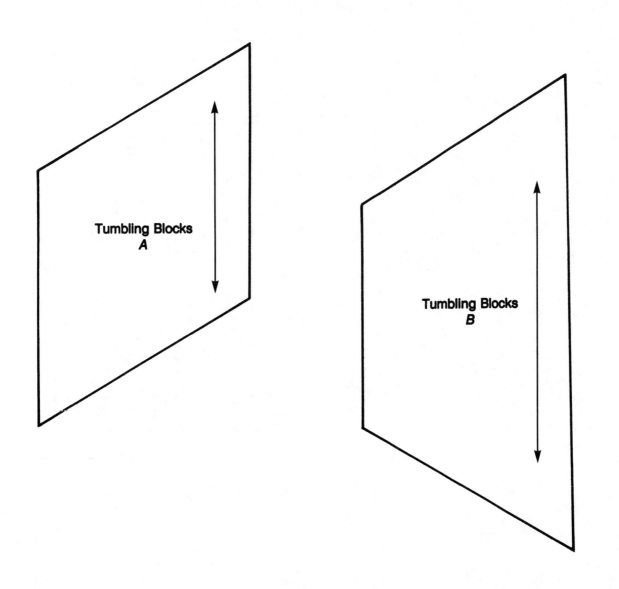

Tumbling Blocks
A

Tumbling Blocks
B

TUMBLING BLOCKS
DESIGN PAGE

For a quick reference or design-your-own:
1. Copy this page.
2. Trim copy to desired quilt size.
3. Color design.

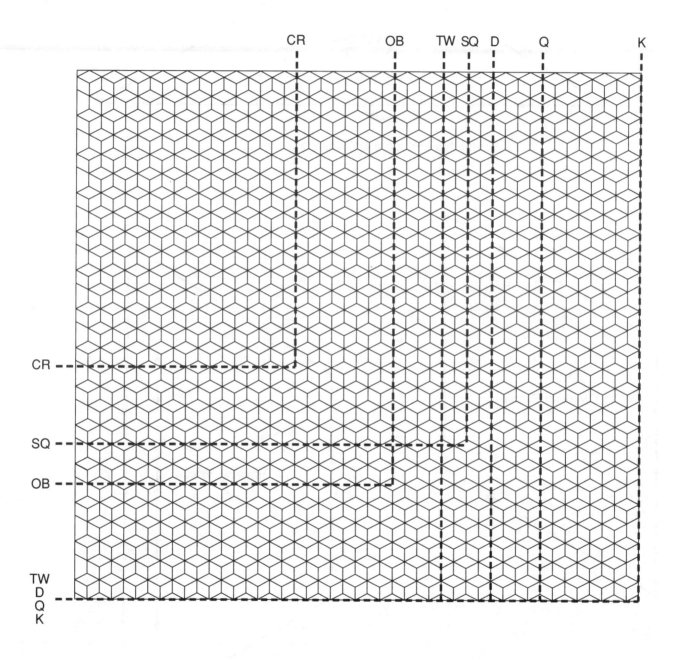

8. BOW TIE
BEGINNER

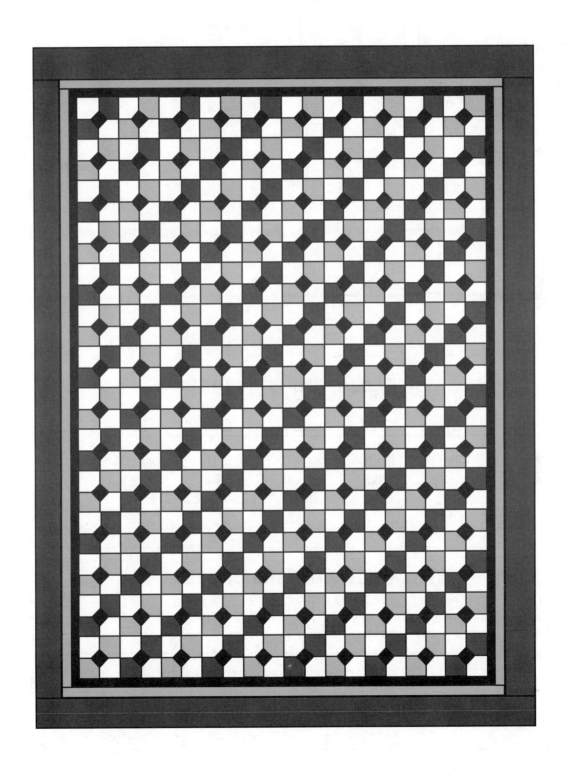

To Speed-Cut:
A. Lop-eared Square
B. Square

Piecing
A. Piecing basic units:

Step 1. Center A piece on B piece (Fig. 1). With B on top, stitch, stopping 1/4″ from each edge of B (Fig. 2).

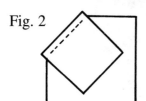
Fig. 2

Step 2. Repeat Step 1 on opposite side of B piece (Fig. 3).

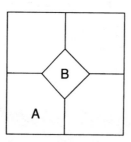
Fig. 1

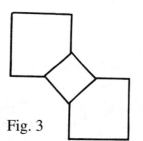
Fig. 3

Step 3. With B on top, add remaining A pieces (Fig. 4).

Step 4. Join A pieces (Fig. 5).

B. Join units.

C. Add borders.

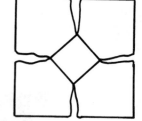

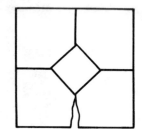
Fig. 4

Finishing
A. Quilt as desired.
B. Bind edges.

Fig. 5

	CR	TW	D	Q	K	SQ	OB
Finished Quilt	48x60	70x106	84x108	86x110	108x108	64x64	60x72
Center	36x48	48x84	60x84	60x84	84x84	48x48	48x60
Border 1	1-1/2	1/2	1-1/2	1-1/2	1-1/2	1-1/2	1-1/2
Border 2	4-1/2	2-1/2	2-1/2	3	2-1/2	6-1/2	4-1/2
Border 3	-	7	8	8-1/2	8	-	-

Number Needed

A - Fabrics 1 & 2 (each)	48	112	140	140	196	64	80
A - Fabric 3 (background)	96	224	280	280	392	128	160
B - Fabric 4	48	112	140	140	196	64	80
Cut Widths							
Border 1	2″	2″	2″	2″	2″	2″	2″
Border 2	6″	3″	3″	3-1/2″	3″	8″	6″
Border 3	-	8-1/2″	9-1/2″	10″	9-1/2″	-	-

For additional information on cutting borders, see page 73.

GENERAL INFORMATION

	CR	TW	D	Q	K	SQ	OB
Blocks Across	6	8	10	10	14	8	8
Blocks Down	8	14	14	14	14	8	10
Total	48	112	140	140	196	64	80

YARDAGES

	CR	TW	D	Q	K	SQ	OB
A - Fabric 1 (bow 1)	3/4	1-1/4	1-1/2	1-1/2	2	3/4	1
A - Fabric 2 (bow 2)	3/4	1-1/4	1-1/2	1-1/2	2	3/4	1
A - Fabric 3 (background)	1-1/4	2-1/4	2-3/4	2-3/4	3-3/4	1-1/2	1-3/4
B - Fabric 4 (knot)	1/2	1-1/8	1-1/4	1-1/4	1-1/4	7/8	7/8
Border 1	1/2	1/2	3/4	3/4	7/8	1/2	1/2
Border 2	1-1/2	1	1-1/8	1-1/2	1-1/4	1-3/4	1-1/2
Border 3	-	2-1/8	2-1/2	3	2-3/4	-	-
Backing	3	6-1/4	8	8-1/4	9-3/4	4	3-3/4

For additional information on yardages, see page 73.

OPTIONS

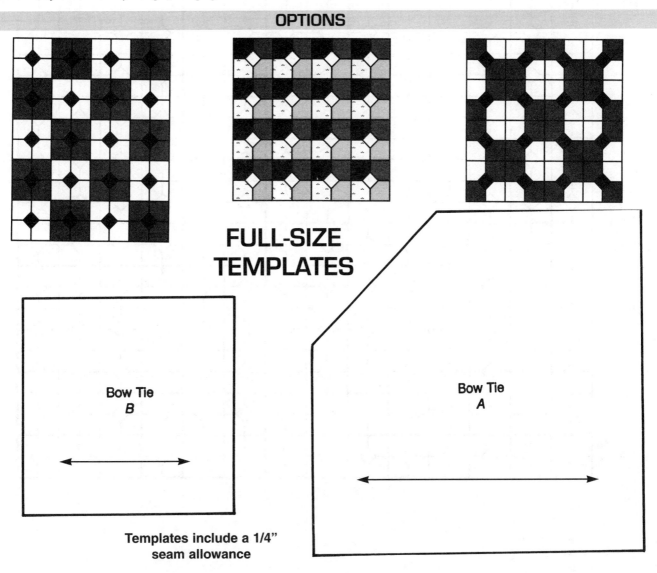

FULL-SIZE TEMPLATES

Bow Tie
B

Bow Tie
A

**Templates include a 1/4"
seam allowance**

BOW TIE
DESIGN PAGE

For a quick reference or design-your-own:
1. Copy this page.
2. Trim copy to desired quilt size.
3. Color design.

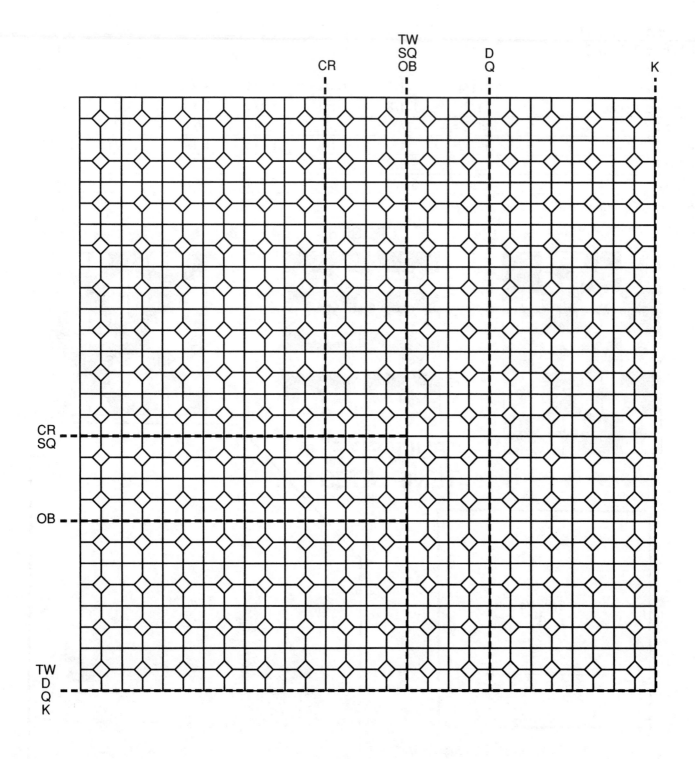

9. FLOATING STARS
BEGINNER

To Speed-Cut:
A. Hexagon
B. Triangle, 60°
Note: I find it helps to copy the design page and refer to it as needed.

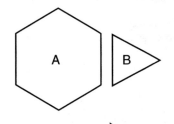

Piecing
A. Piecing units:

Step 1. Sew B units to A unit as shown (Fig. 1). Press to triangles.

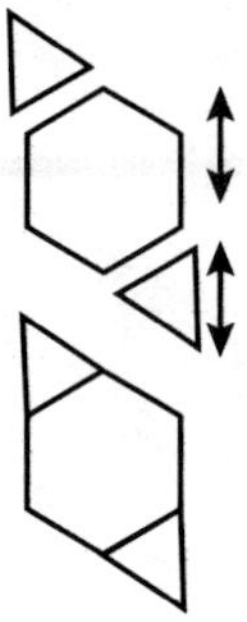

Step 2. Sew B unit to A as shown for outer rows (Fig. 2).

NOTE: The grainline as shown will help in stitching the columns together. I try to keep them in this direction as much as possible.

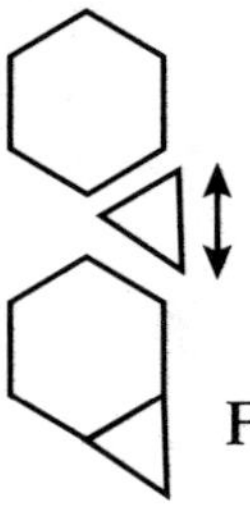

B. Sewing units into columns:

Step 1. Sew short columns, press down (Fig. 3).

Step 2. Sew long columns, press up (Fig. 4).

Step 3. Sew the first and last columns (Fig. 5).

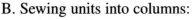

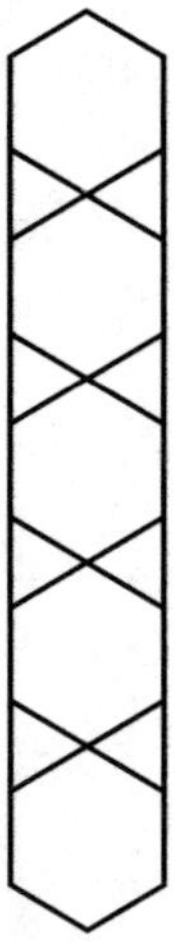

Fig. 1

Fig. 2

Fig. 3

Fig. 4

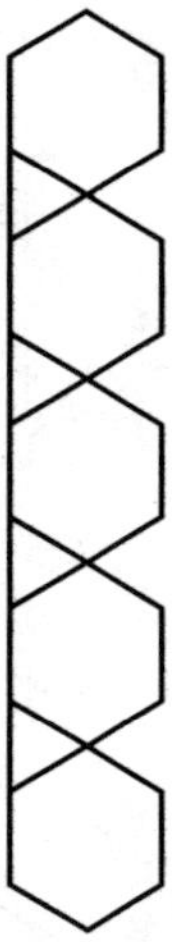

Fig. 5

C. Joining the columns:

Step 1. Sew columns together (Fig. 6). Use the "tabs" from the seams to help in matching. If needed, turn the tabs until the match is made, then turn them back in place.

D. Trim edges as shown (Fig. 7). Be sure to leave 1/4″ extra for seam allowance.

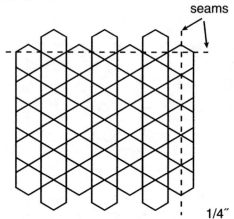

Fig. 6

seams

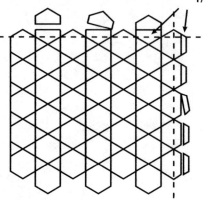

1/4″ Fig. 7

E. Add borders.

Finishing
A. Quilt as desired.
B. Bind edges.

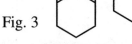

DIMENSIONS (INCHES)

	CR	TW	D	Q	K	SQ	OB
Finished Size	50x58	72x104	83x106	92x106	107x113	64x70	58x72
Center	40x48	54x86	63x86	72x86	86x90	56x62	48x62
Border 1	1-1/2	2	1-1/2	2	2	1	1-1/2
Border 2	1-1/2	2	2	2	2	1	1-1/2
Border 3	2	5	6-1/2	6	7	2	2

CUTTING INSTRUCTIONS

	CR	TW	D	Q	K	SQ	OB
Number Needed							
A - Fabric 1	126	227	262	297	367	217	188
B - Fabric 2	210	396	504	594	702	414	324
Cut Widths							
Border 1	2″	2-1/2″	2″	2-1/2″	2-1/2″	1-1/2″	2″
Border 2	2″	2-1/2″	2-1/2″	2-1/2″	2-1/2″	1-1/2″	2″
Border 3	3-1/2″	6-1/2″	8″	7-1/2″	8-1/2″	3-1/2″	3-1/2″

For additional information on cutting borders, see page 73.

GENERAL INFORMATION

	CR	TW	D	Q	K	SQ	OB
Units Across (Columns)	11	13	15	17	21	15	13
Units Down (Odd-No. Column)	11	17	17	17	17	14	14
Units Down (Even-No. Column)	12	18	18	18	18	15	15
Total	126	227	262	297	367	217	188

YARDAGES

	CR	TW	D	Q	K	SQ	OB
A - Fabric 1	2-1/4	6	7	8	9-1/2	4-1/2	3-3/4
A - Fabric 2	1-1/8	2	2-1/4	2-3/4	3-1/4	1-3/4	1-1/2
Border 1	1/2	3/4	3/4	1	1	1/2	1/2
Border 2	3/4	1	1	1	1-1/4	1/2	3/4
Border 3	7/8	2	2-3/4	2-1/2	3	1	1
Backing	3	6-1/4	8	8-1/2	10-3/4	4	3-3/4

For additional information on yardages, see page 73.

OPTIONS

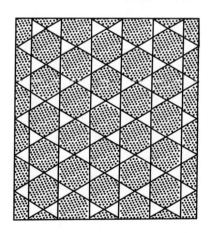
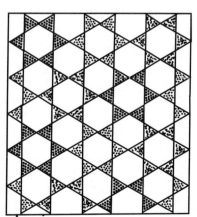
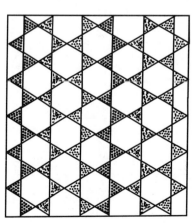

FULL-SIZE TEMPLATES

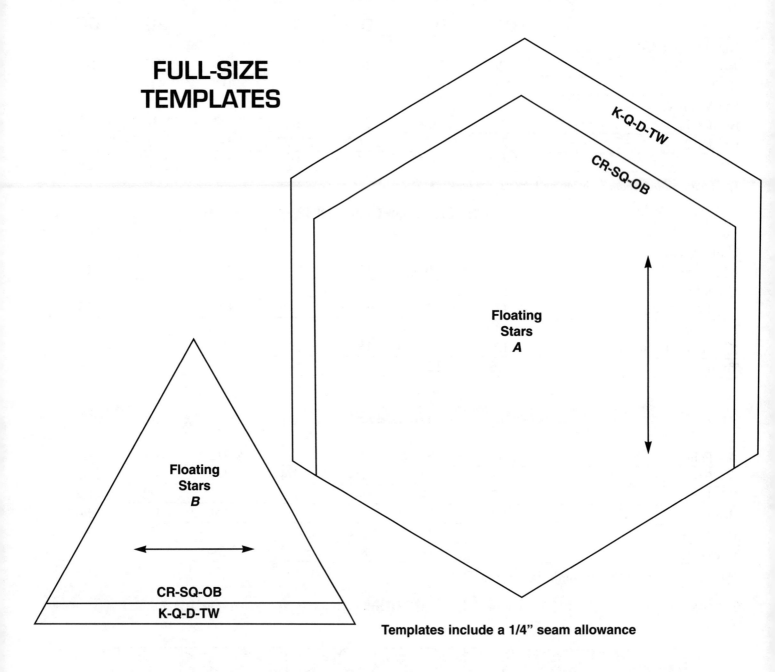

K-Q-D-TW

CR-SQ-OB

**Floating
Stars
A**

**Floating
Stars
B**

CR-SQ-OB

K-Q-D-TW

Templates include a 1/4" seam allowance

FLOATING STARS
DESIGN PAGE

For a quick reference or design-your-own:
1. Copy this page.
2. Trim copy to desired quilt size.
3. Color design.

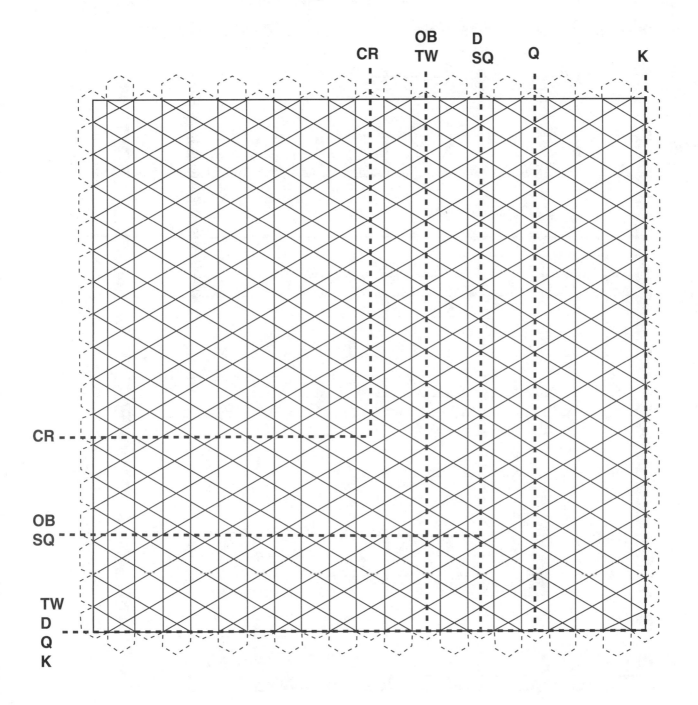

10. PINEY WOODS
BEGINNER

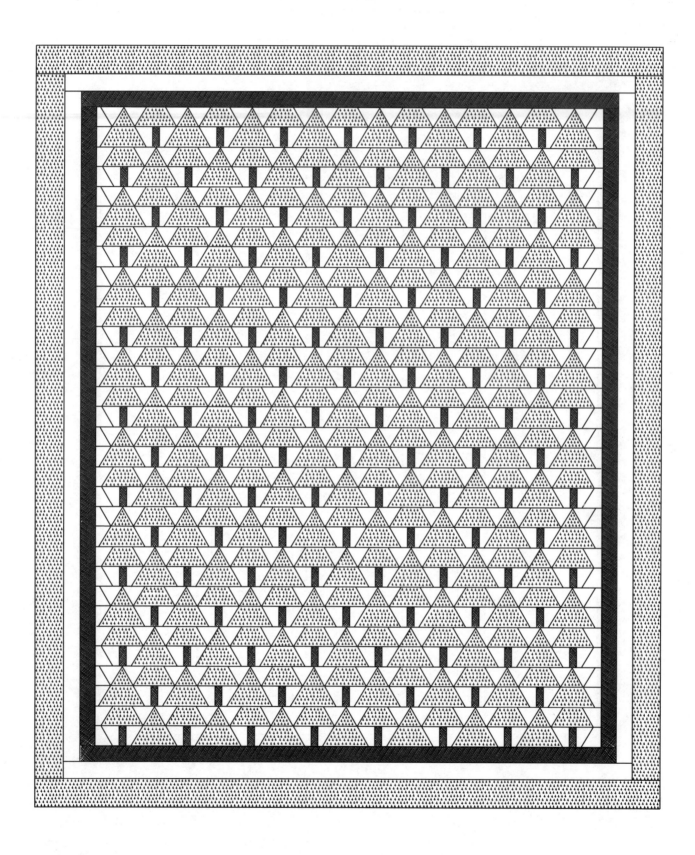

To Speed-Cut:

A. Wedge, 60°
B. Triangle, 60°

Piecing

A Piecing the tree trunks:

Step 1. Stitch strips as shown (Fig. 1). Press seams toward trunk.

Step 2. Cut 2-1/4″ units from this strip (Fig. 2). *Step 3.* Cut A pieces from these units (Fig. 3).

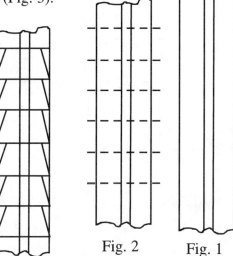

Fig. 3   Fig. 2   Fig. 1

B. Piecing rows:

Step 1. Stitch rows as shown (Fig. 4). End pieces are one background A piece, cut in half (Fig. 5). Press toward

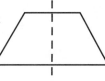

Fig. 5

tree pieces (exception: when sewing three B pieces together, press second seam away from tree).

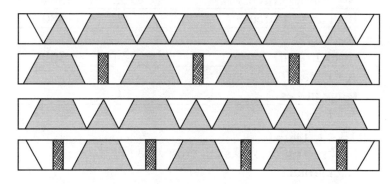

Fig. 4

Step 2. Repeat these 4 rows.

Step 3. Trim side edges, if needed.

C. Stitch rows together, centering tree trunks to tips of trees. Press seams down.

D. Add borders.

Finishing

A. Quilt as desired.
B. Bind edges.

DIMENSIONS (INCHES)

	CR	TW	D	Q	K	SQ	OB
Finished Size	49x59	71x106	86x108	88x110	105x108	63x65	61x72
Center	37x47	49x84	62x84	62x84	81x84	47x49	49x60
Border 1	1-1/2	1-1/2	1-1/2	1-1/2	1-1/2	1-1/2	1-1/2
Border 2	4-1/2	2-1/2	2-1/2	3	2-1/2	6-1/2	4-1/2
Border 3	-	7	8	8-1/2	8	-	-

CUTTING INSTRUCTIONS

	CR	TW	D	Q	K	SQ	OB
Number Needed							
A - Fabric 1 (trees)	162	384	480	480	624	216	272
B - Fabric 1 (trees)	77	180	228	228	300	105	128
B - Fabric 2 (background)	154	360	456	456	600	210	256
A - Fabric 2 (edge pieces)	14	24	24	24	24	14	18
A - Fabric 3 Tree Trunk Unit	77	180	228	228	300	105	128
Strips to make trunks cut crosswise (42″ fabric)							
Background cut 2-1/2″ wide	10	22	28	28	36	14	16
Trunk Fabric cut 1-1/2″ wide	5	11	14	14	18	7	8
Cut Widths							
Border 1	2″	2″	2″	2″	2″	2″	2″
Border 2	6″	3″	3″	3-1/2″	3″	8″	6″
Border 3	-	8-1/2″	9-1/2″	10″	9-1/2″	-	-

For additional information on cutting borders, see page 73.

GENERAL INFORMATION

	CR	TW	D	Q	K	SQ	OB
Trees Across (one row)	6	8	10	10	13	8	8
Rows Down	27	48	48	48	48	27	34
Total Trees	77	180	228	228	300	105	128

YARDAGES

	CR	TW	D	Q	K	SQ	OB
Fabric 1 (trees)	1-5/8	3-1/4	4	4	5-1/4	2	2-1/2
Fabric 2 (background)	1-1/2	3	4	4	4-3/4	2-1/8	2-1/2
Fabric 3 (tree trunks)	1/4	5/8	3/4	3/4	7/8	3/8	3/8
Border 1	1/2	1/2	3/4	3/4	7/8	1/2	1/2
Border 2	1-1/2	1	1-1/8	1-1/2	1-1/4	1-3/4	1-1/2
Border 3	-	2-1/8	2-1/2	3	2-3/4	-	-
Backing	3	6-1/4	8	8-1/4	9-3/4	4	3-3/4

For additional information on yardages, see page 73.

FULL-SIZE TEMPLATES

Templates include a 1/4" seam allowance

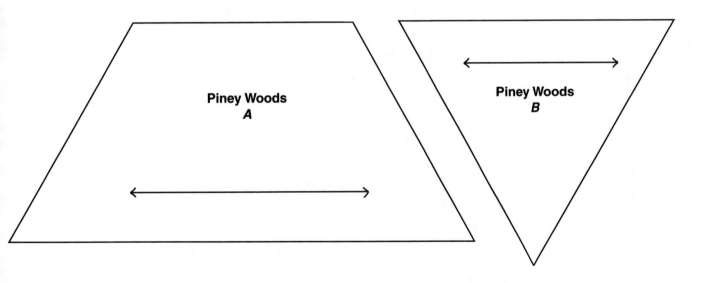

Piney Woods
A

Piney Woods
B

PINEY WOODS
DESIGN PAGE

For a quick reference or design-your-own:
1. Copy this page.
2. Trim copy to desired quilt size.
3. Color design.

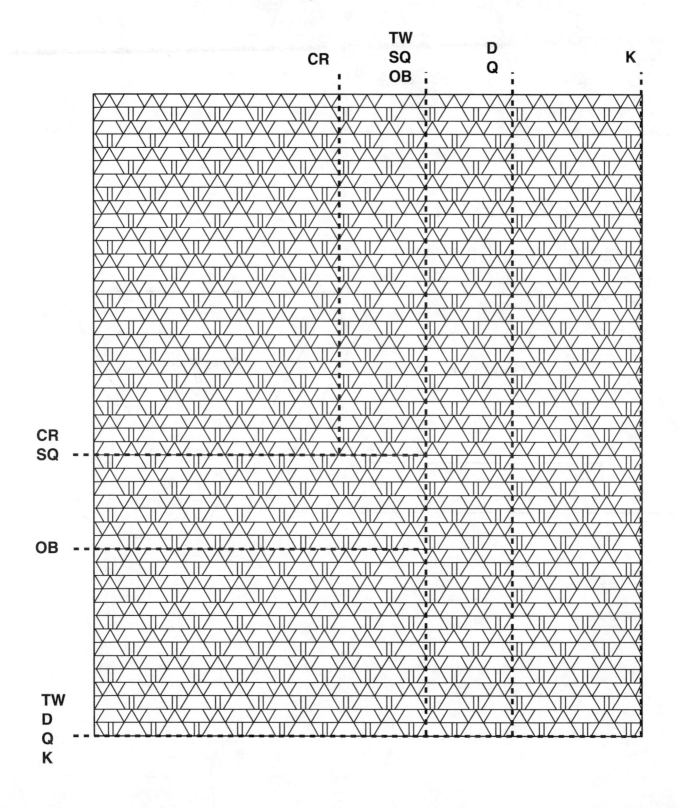

11. ALWAYS FRIENDS
INTERMEDIATE

To Speed-Cut:
A. Applecore

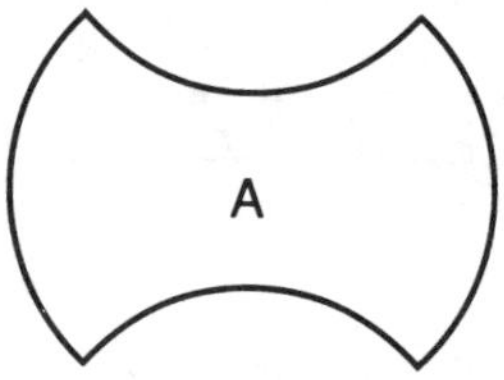

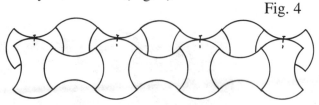

Piecing

A. Piecing Units:

Step 1. Center curved sections as shown (Fig. 1). Pin at center point.

Step 2. Turn unit over so inner curve is now on top (Fig. 2). Stitch.

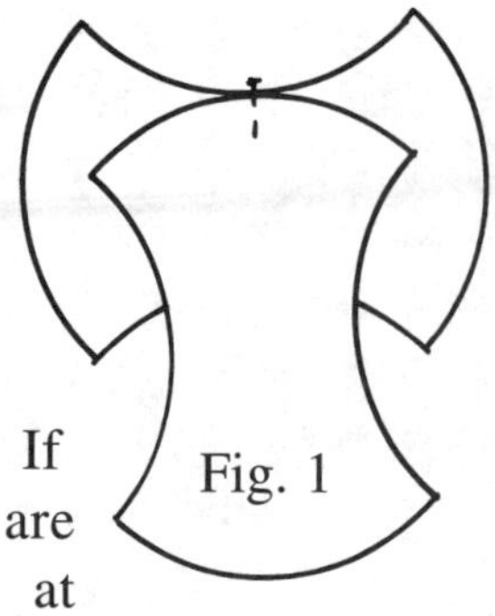

Fig. 1

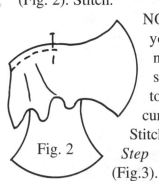

NOTE: If you are new at sewing curved seams, refer to the section about sewing curved seams in Chapter 5. Stitch a few practice pieces first!

Fig. 2

Step 3. Join pieces in rows (Fig.3).

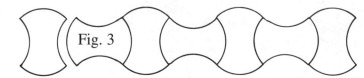

Fig. 3

NOTE: There is no need to clip these curved seams because the "puckery" look will be absorbed in the quilting.

B. Joining the rows:

Step 1. Place two rows together, pinning centers of every other curve (Fig. 4).

Fig. 4

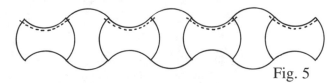

Step 2. Stitch **pinned curves only**, starting and ending about 1/4″ past each seam (Fig. 5). (I find it easier and faster to pin the seams, too.)

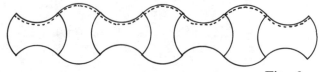

Fig. 5

Step 3. Turn piece over. Stitch remaining portions of seam (Fig. 6).

Fig. 6

Finishing

A. Quilt as desired.

B. Cut bias binding 2-1/4″ wide. Bind, following curved edges.

DIMENSIONS (INCHES)

	CR	TW	D	Q	K	SQ	OB
Finished Quilt	36x52	73x102	86x102	92x108	105x108	67x71	61x77

CUTTING INSTRUCTIONS

Number Needed A - Fabrics 1 & 2 (each)	CR	TW	D	Q	K	SQ	OB
		94	380	446	508	578	242	238
Binding	Cut bias 2-1/4″ wide						

GENERAL INFORMATION

Blocks Across	11	23	27	29	33	21	19
Blocks Down	17	33	33	35	35	23	25
Total	187	759	891	1015	1155	483	475

YARDAGES

A - Fabric 1 (dark)	1-3/4	5-3/4	6-3/4	7-5/8	8-5/8	3-7/8	3-7/8
A - Fabric 2 (light)	1-3/4	5-3/4	6-3/4	7-5/8	8-5/8	3-7/8	3-7/8
Backing	1-5/8	6-1/4	7-3/4	8-1/4	10	4-1/4	3-3/4
Binding	3/4	1-1/8	1-1/4	1-1/4	1-1/2	1	1

For additional information on yardages, see page 73.

OPTIONS

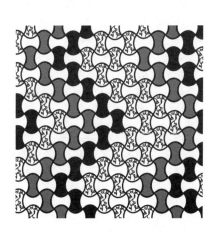

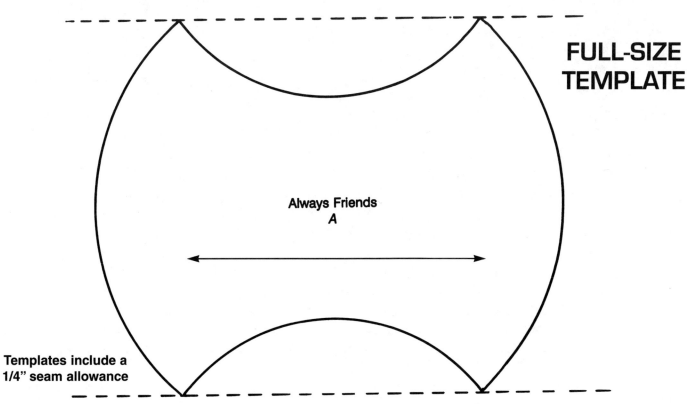

FULL-SIZE TEMPLATE

Always Friends
A

**Templates include a
1/4" seam allowance**

ALWAYS FRIENDS
DESIGN PAGE

For a quick reference or design-your-own:
1. Copy this page.
2. Trim copy to desired quilt size.
3. Color design.

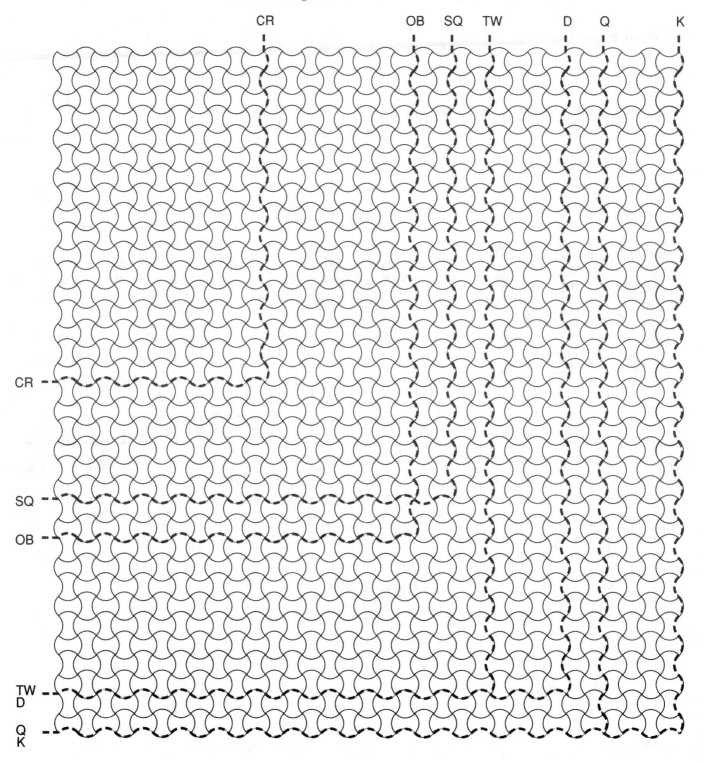

12. MAGNOLIAS
INTERMEDIATE

To Speed-Cut:

A, C, E. Square

D. Rectangle

B. Triangle, 45° and Clipped Points

Squares for Edge Triangles: Cut 9″ x 9″, cut in half diagonally.

Squares for Corner Triangles: Cut 6-1/2″ x 6-1/2″, cut diagonally in both directions.

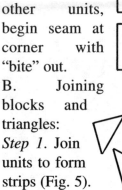

Cutting Notes: The B pieces are mirror images. Stack fabrics with like sides together.

Piecing

A. Piecing blocks:

  Step 1. Join B pieces, matching clipped points to square corners (Fig. 1).

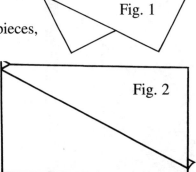

Fig. 1

  NOTE: When pressing, you'll see a tiny "bite" out of each corner (Fig. 2). These are rather strange-looking units, but they work—your triangles will match like magic!

Fig. 2

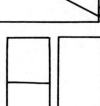

Fig. 3

Step 2. Join bud units (Fig. 3).

Step 3. Join units (Fig. 4).

NOTE: When stitching triangle units to other units, begin seam at corner with "bite" out.

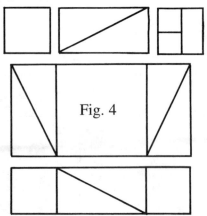

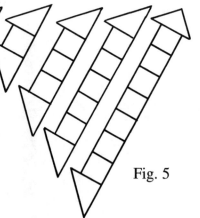

Fig. 4

B. Joining blocks and triangles:

Step 1. Join units to form strips (Fig. 5).

Step 2. Join strips.

C. Add borders.

Finishing

A. Quilt as desired.

B. Bind edges.

Fig. 5

DIMENSIONS (INCHES)

	CR	TW	D	Q	K	SQ	OB
Finished Quilt	43x55	70x104	84x106	88x110	108x108	65x65	57x80
Center	33x45	56x90	68x90	68x90	90x90	45x45	45x68
Border 1	1-1/2	2	1-1/2	1-1/2	1-1/2	1-1/2	2
Border 2	3-1/2	5	2-1/2	3	3	3	4
Border 3	-	-	4	5-1/2	4-1/2	5-1/2	-

CUTTING INSTRUCTIONS

	CR	TW	D	Q	K	SQ	OB
A - Fabric 2	18	68	83	83	113	25	39
B - Fabric 2 & 3 (each)	36	136	166	166	226	50	78
B - Fabric 4	72	272	332	332	452	100	156
C - Fabric 4	54	204	249	249	339	75	117
D - Fabric 4	18	68	83	83	113	25	39
E - Fabric 1 & 4 (each)	18	68	83	83	113	25	39
Edge Triangles Fabric 4	10	22	24	24	28	12	16
Corner Triangles Fabric 4	4	4	4	4	4	4	4
Cut Widths Border 1	2″	2-1/2″	2″	2″	2″	2″	2-1/2″
Border 2	5″	6-1/2″	3″	3-1/2″	3-1/2″	3-1/2″	5-1/2″
Border 3	-	-	5-1/2″	7″	6″	7″	-

For additional information on cutting borders, see page 73.

GENERAL INFORMATION

	CR	TW	D	Q	K	SQ	OB
Blocks Across	3	5	6	6	8	4	4
Blocks Down	4	8	8	8	8	4	6
Total	18	68	83	83	113	25	39

YARDAGES

	CR	TW	D	Q	K	SQ	OB
E - Fabric 1 (bud "center")	1/8	1/8	1/4	1/4	1/4	1/8	1/8
A & B - Fabric 2 (Magnolia)	1	2-1/4	2-3/4	2-3/4	3-1/2	1-1/4	1-1/2
B - Fabric 3 (Leaves)	3/8	1	1-1/4	1-1/4	1-1/2	1/2	5/8
B, C, D, E - Fabric 4 (Background)	1-1/4	3-1/4	4	4	5-1/2	1-3/4	2
Triangles - Fabric 4	3/4	1	1-1/4	1-1/4	1-1/2	3/4	1
Border 1	1/2	3/4	3/4	3/4	3/4	3/4	3/4
Border 2	1-1/4	2	1	1-1/4	1-1/2	1	1-1/2
Border 3	-	-	2	2-1/4	2-1/2	2	-
Backing	3	6-1/2	7-3/4	8-3/4	10-1/2	4-1/4	3-3/4

For additional information on yardages, see page 73.

FULL-SIZE TEMPLATES

Magnolias
E

Magnolias
A

**Cut diagonally to make triangles
Cut squares for:
Edges: 9 x 9
Corners: 6-1/2 x 6-1/2**

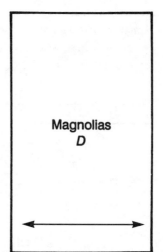

Magnolias
D

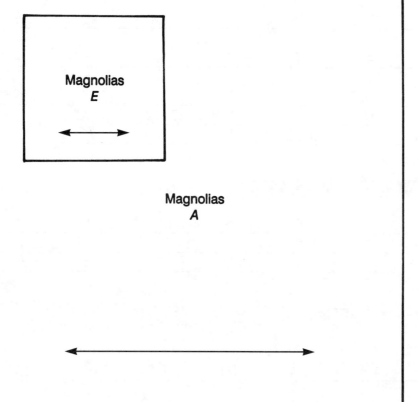

**Templates include a
1/4" seam allowance**

Magnolias
B

Note: Reverse half of B pieces (cut mirror image)

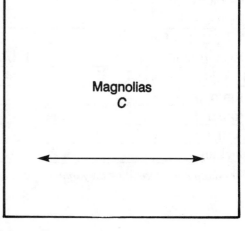

Magnolias
C

MAGNOLIAS
DESIGN PAGE

For a quick reference or design-your-own:
1. Copy this page.
2. Trim copy to desired quilt size.
3. Color design.

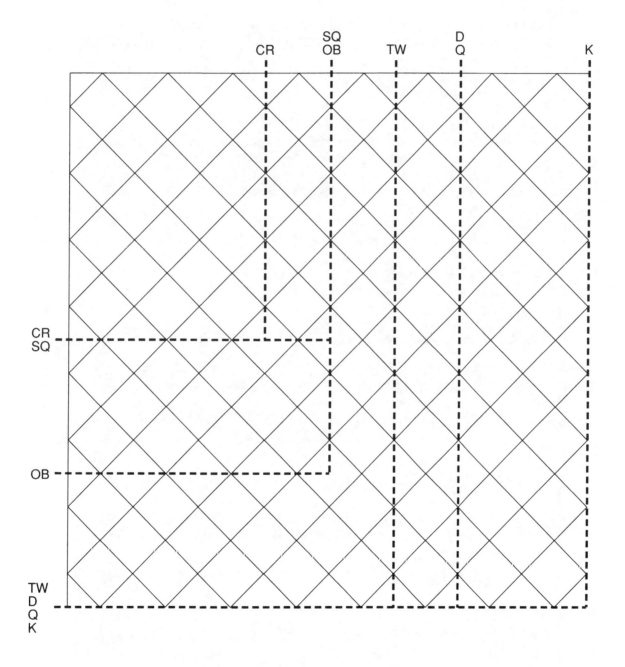

13. CLAMSHELL
INTERMEDIATE

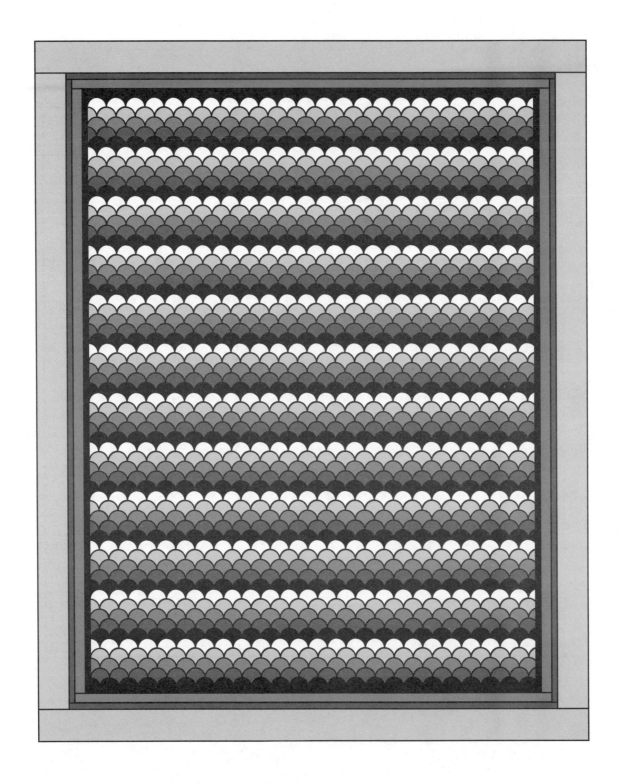

To Speed-Cut:

A. Archway

NOTE: The Clamshell quilt is pieced from the top down. It begins with a 4-1/2″ wide strip across the entire top of the quilt. This is the starting strip and is used as a base on which to sew the first row of clamshells. The quilt is then built, row by row, down from there.

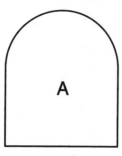

Piecing

A. Piecing the shells:

Step 1. Join shell in rows 1″ up from base (Fig. 1).

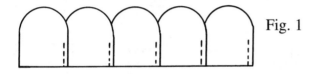

Fig. 1

Step 2. With running stitch and pressing template, prepare rounded edges for appliqué. Press seams open (Fig. 2).

Fig. 2

Step 3. Matching base of first shell row to base of starting strip, and centering shell unit on strip, pin in place (Fig. 3). Baste curved edges.

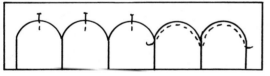

Fig. 3

Step 4. Using transparent ruler, mark 1-5/8″ from bottom edge of basted strip. Mark only a **tiny** point at shell joining (Fig. 4).

Fig. 4

1-5/8″

NOTE: The shells must meet neatly at this point. If they do not, adjust in final appliqué.

Step 5. Pin and baste row 2, matching center top of each shell with mark on previous row (Fig. 5).

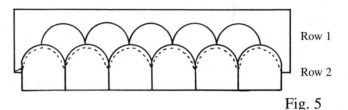

Row 1

Row 2

Fig. 5

NOTE: The even-numbered rows will have an extra half-shell at each end. Appliqué **only** from **center top** of these shells (Fig. 6).

Start appliqué

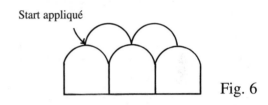

Fig. 6

Step 6. Hand or machine appliqué row 1. Trim away seams on back of row. (On row 1 you'll be trimming away a bit of the starting strip, too.)

Step 7. Repeat Steps 4, 5, and 6.

NOTE: When measuring 1-5/8″ in Step 4, check previous rows to be sure they are even and parallel with the newest row.

B. Trimming sides: Trim away excess shells from sides, leaving 1/4″ seam allowance.

C. Add border.

Finishing

A. Quilt as desired.

B. Bind edges.

DIMENSIONS (INCHES)

	CR	TW	D	Q	K	SQ	OB
Finished Quilt	42x57	70x103	84x104	91x106	106x106	67x67	59x74
Center	30x45	50x83	60x80	65x80	80x80	55x55	43x58
Border 1	2	1-1/2	1-1/2	1-1/2	1-1/2	2	1-1/2
Border 2	4	3	3	4	4	4	2-1/2
Border 3	-	5-1/2	1-1/2	1-1/2	1-1/2	-	4
Border 4	-	-	6	6	6	-	-

For additional information on cutting borders, see page 73.

CUTTING INSTRUCTIONS

A - Fabrics 1-5 (dark to light)

	CR	TW	D	Q	K	SQ	OB
(each)	104	294	325	338	832	207	180
Cut Starter Strip (top row)	4-1/2x40	4-1/2x60	4-1/2x70	4-1/2x75	4-1/2x168	4-1/2x65	4-1/2x53
Cut Widths							
Border 1	2-1/2″	2″	2″	2″	2″	2-1/2″	2″
Border 2	5-1/2″	3-1/2″	3-1/2″	4-1/2″	4-1/2″	5-1/2″	3″
Border 3	-	7″	2″	2″	2″	-	5-1/2″
Border 4	-	-	7-1/2″	7-1/2″	7-1/2″	-	-

GENERAL INFORMATION

	CR	TW	D	Q	K	SQ	OB
Shells Across	12	20	24	26	32	22	17
Shells Down (rows)	36	66	64	64	64	44	46
Total	450	1353	1568	1696	4064	990	805

YARDAGES

A - Fabrics 1-5

	CR	TW	D	Q	K	SQ	OB
(each)	1	2-1/4	2-1/2	2-5/8	6	1-3/4	1-3/8
Starter Strip	1/4	3/8	3/8	3/8	3/4	3/8	3/8
Border 1	3/4	3/4	3/4	3/4	3/4	3/4	1/2
Border 2	1-1/2	1	1-1/4	1-1/2	1-3/4	1-1/2	3/4
Border 3	-	2	3/4	3/4	3/4	-	1-1/2
Border 4	-	-	2-1/2	2-1/2	3	-	-
Backing	3-1/4	6-3/4	8-1/2	8-1/2	10-1/4	4	3-3/4

For additional information on yardages, see page 73.

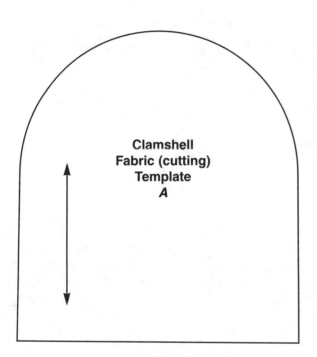

FULL-SIZE TEMPLATES

Cutting templates include a 1/4" seam allowance

Clamshell Fabric (cutting) Template *A*

Clamshell Pressing Template *A*

CLAMSHELL
DESIGN PAGE

For a quick reference or design-your-own:
1. Copy this page.
2. Trim copy to desired quilt size.
3. Color design.

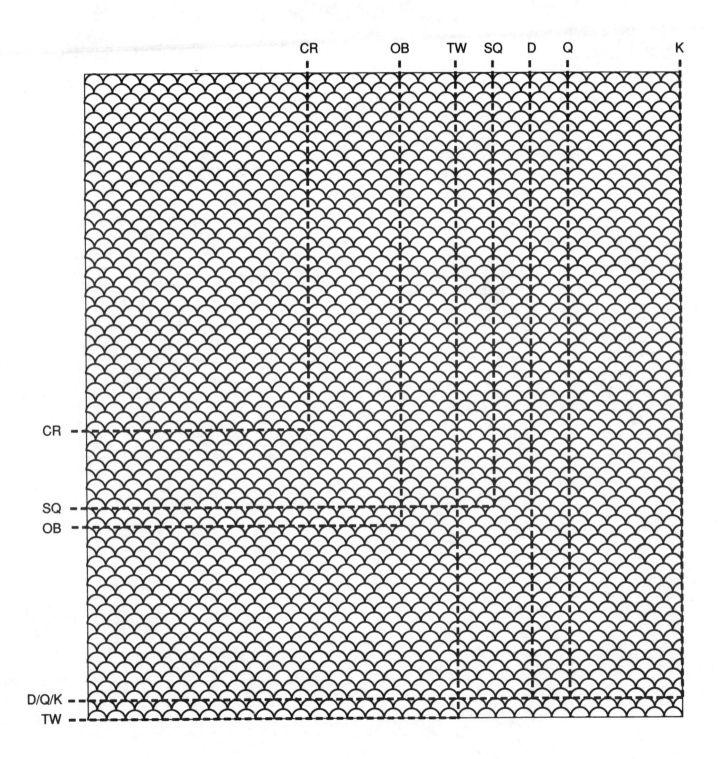

14. LOVE RING
INTERMEDIATE

To Speed-Cut:
A. Bite
B. Fan

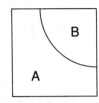

Piecing
A. Piecing basic units:

Step 1. Center piece B on Piece A. Pin at center (Fig. 1).
Step 2. With A on top, stitch from one edge to the pin

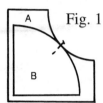

Fig. 1

(Fig. 2). With needle in fabric, match corners. Finish stitching seam (Fig. 3). You may want to pin the ends if you have trouble keeping them lined up. (If you are new to curved piecing, see Sewing Curves, page 35.)

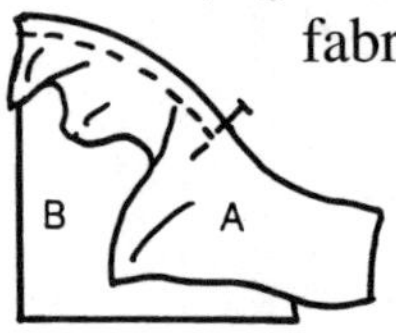

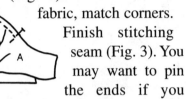

Fig. 2

Fig. 3

NOTE: There is no need to clip these curved seams because the "puckery" look will be absorbed in the quilting.

B. Joining the units:
Step 1. Join 4 units to form the three squares needed (Fig. 4).
Step 2. Using the picture shown on page 133, join the squares (Fig. 5).

Fig. 4

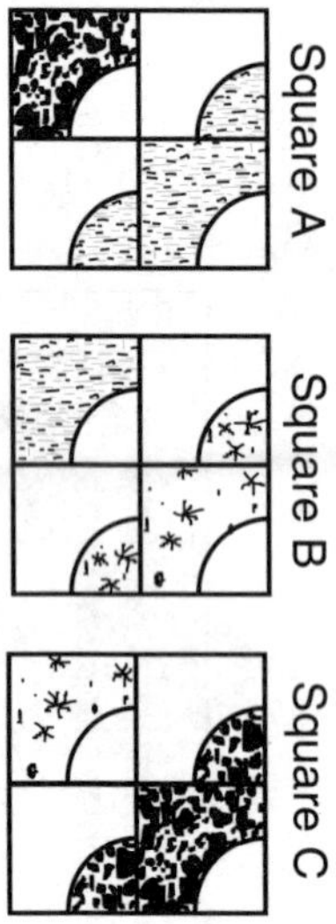

Square A

Square B

Square C

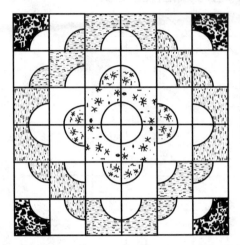

C. Add borders.

Fig. 5

Finishing
A. Quilt as desired.
B. Bind edges.

DIMENSIONS (INCHES)

	CR	TW	D	Q	K	SQ	OB
Finished Quilt	48x60	70x102	86x102	90x106	106x106	64x64	60x72
Center	36x48	48x80	64x80	64x80	80x80	48x48	48x60
Border 1	2	1-1/2	1-1/2	1-1/2	1-1/2	1-1/2	2
Border 2	4	3	3	4	4	2-1/2	4
Border 3	-	1-1/2	1-1/2	1-1/2	1-1/2	4	-
Border 4	-	5	5	6	6	-	-

CUTTING INSTRUCTIONS

	CR	TW	D	Q	K	SQ	OB
(Note: CR, SQ, OB are 3″ units; TW, D, Q are 4″ units; K is a 5″ unit. Four units are one block.)							
A, B - (each) Fabric 1 (Background)	96	120	160	160	128	128	160
*A - Fabrics 2, 3, 4 (each)	32	40	56	56	48	48	56
*B - Fabrics 2, 3, 4 (each)	32	40	56	56	48	48	56
Cut Widths							
Border 1	2-1/2″	2″	2″	2″	2″	2″	2-1/2″
Border 2	5-1/2″	3-1/2″	3-1/2″	4-1/2″	4-1/2″	3″	5-1/2″
Border 3	-	2″	2″	2″	2″	5-1/2″	-
Border 4	-	6-1/2″	6-1/2″	7-1/2″	7-1/2″	-	-
Blocks Needed							
Block A	16	20	28	28	20	20	28
Block B	16	20	28	28	24	24	28
Block C	16	20	24	24	20	20	24

For additional information on cutting borders, see page 73.

*There will be several pieces remaining on the D, Q, K, SQ, OB. (Trust me; it's less confusing this way!)

GENERAL INFORMATION

	CR	TW	D	Q	K	SQ	OB
Blocks Across	6	6	8	8	8	8	8
Blocks Down	8	10	10	10	8	8	10
Total	48	60	80	80	64	64	80

YARDAGES

	CR	TW	D	Q	K	SQ	OB
Fabric 1 (Background)	1-1/2	3	3-3/4	3-3/4	5	2	2-1/2
Fabrics 2, 3, 4 (each)	5/8	1-1/4	1-1/2	1-1/2	2	1-3/4	1
Border 1	3/4	3/4	3/4	3/4	3/4	3/4	3/4
Border 2	1-1/2	1	1-1/4	1-1/2	2	1	1-1/2
Border 3	-	3/4	3/4	3/4	3/4	1-1/2	-
Border 4	-	2	2-1/4	2-1/2	3	-	-
Backing	3-1/4	6-3/4	8-1/2	8-1/2	10-1/4	4	3-3/4

For additional information on yardages, see page 73.

*This option is the Drunkard's Path

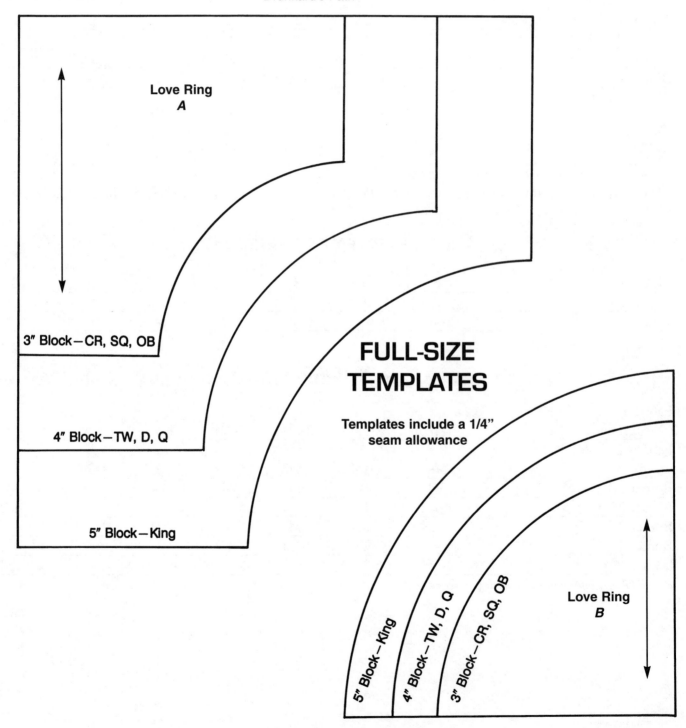

Love Ring
A

3" Block—CR, SQ, OB

4" Block—TW, D, Q

5" Block—King

FULL-SIZE TEMPLATES

Templates include a 1/4" seam allowance

5" Block—King

4" Block—TW, D, Q

3" Block—CR, SQ, OB

Love Ring
B

LOVE RING
DESIGN PAGE

For a quick reference or design-your-own:
1. *Copy this page.*
2. *Trim copy to desired quilt size.*
3. *Color design.*

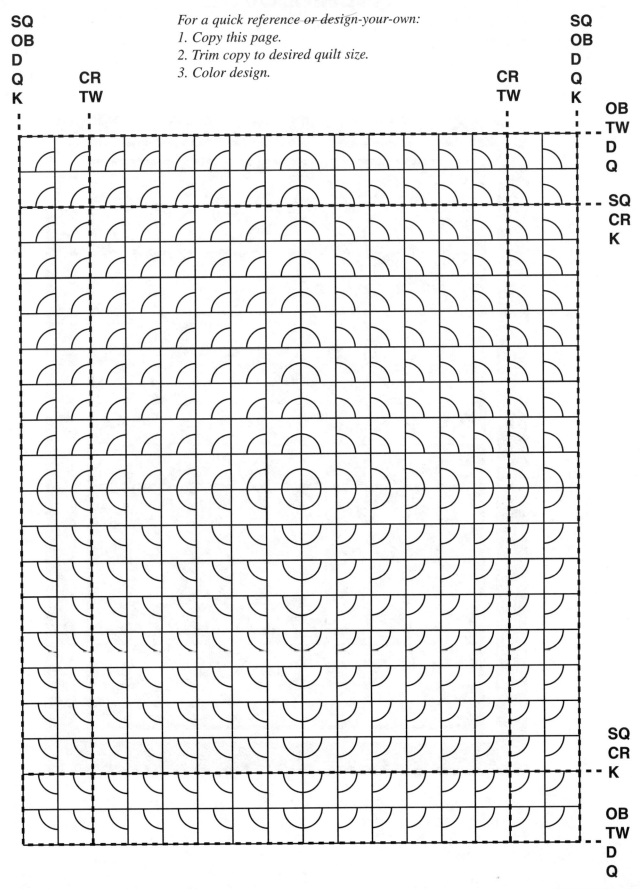

15. INDIAN STAR
INTERMEDIATE

To Speed-Cut:

A. Triangle, 45°
B. Wedge, 45°
C. Diamond, 45°

NOTE: All strips used for B and C must be cut on the lengthwise grain.

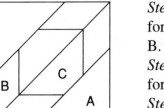

Piecing

A. Piecing basic units:

Step 1. Join B and C pieces, using **bias** edge of C for the seam (Fig. 1).

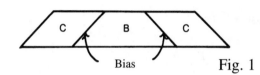

Fig. 1

Step 2. Add A pieces (Fig. 2).

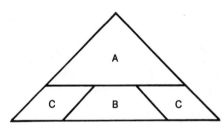

Fig. 2

Step 3. Join triangles to form basic unit (Fig. 3).
B. Joining Units:
Step 1. Join 4 units to form squares (Fig. 4).
Step 2. Sew squares together.
C. Add borders.

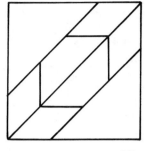

Fig. 3

Finishing

A. Quilt as desired.
B. Bind edges.

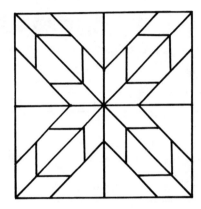

Fig. 4

DIMENSIONS (INCHES)

	CR	TW	D	Q	K	SQ	OB
Finished Quilt	48x60	70x106	84x108	86x110	108x108	64x64	60x72
Center	36x48	48x84	60x84	60x84	84x84	48x48	48x60
Border 1	1-1/2	1-1/2	1-1/2	1-1/2	1-1/2	1-1/2	1-1/2
Border 2	4-1/2	2-1/2	2-1/2	3	2-1/2	6-1/2	4-1/2
Border 3	-	7	8	8-1/2	8	-	-

CUTTING INSTRUCTIONS

	CR	TW	D	Q	K	SQ	OB
Number Needed							
A - Fabrics 1 & 2 (each)	48	112	140	140	196	64	80
B - Fabrics 1 & 2 (each)	96	224	280	280	392	128	160
C - Fabrics 1 & 2 (each)	48	112	140	140	196	64	80
Cut Widths							
Border 1	2″	2″	2″	2″	2″	2″	2″
Border 2	6″	3″	3″	3-1/2″	3″	8″	6″
Border 3	-	8-1/2″	9-1/2″	10″	9-1/2″	-	-

For additional information on cutting borders, see page 73.

GENERAL INFORMATION

	CR	TW	D	Q	K	SQ	OB
Blocks Across	6	8	10	10	14	8	8
Blocks Down	8	14	14	14	14	8	10
Total	48	112	140	140	196	64	80

YARDAGES

	CR	TW	D	Q	K	SQ	OB
Fabric 1 (dark)	2	3-5/8	4-1/2	4-1/2	6-1/8	2-1/4	2-3/4
Fabric 2 (light)	2	3-5/8	4-1/2	4-1/2	6-1/8	2-1/4	2-3/4
Border 1	1/2	1/2	3/4	3/4	7/8	12	1/2
Border 2	1-1/2	1	1-1/8	1-1/2	1-1/4	1-3/4	1-1/2
Border 3	-	2-1/2	3	3-1/4	3-1/2	-	-
Backing	3	6-1/4	8	8-1/4	9-3/4	4	3-3/4

For additional information on yardages, see page 73.

OPTIONS

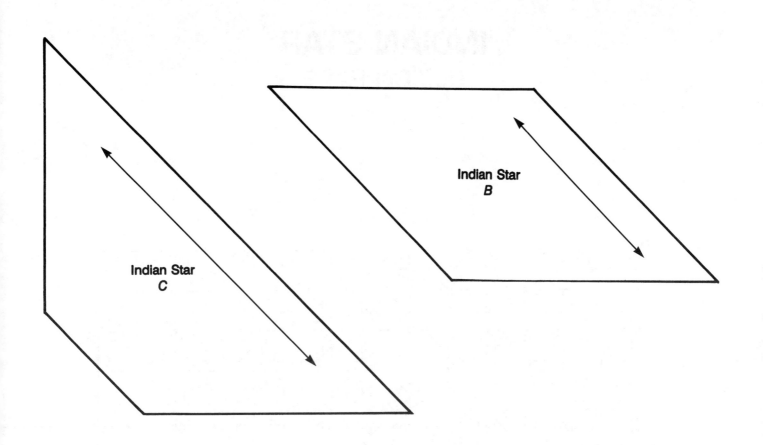

Indian Star
B

Indian Star
C

FULL-SIZE TEMPLATES

Templates include a 1/4" seam allowance

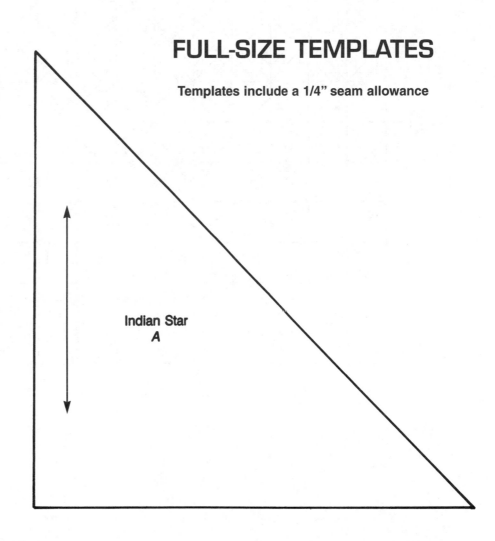

Indian Star
A

INDIAN STAR
DESIGN PAGE

For a quick reference or design-your-own:
1. Copy this page.
2. Trim copy to desired quilt size.
3. Color design.

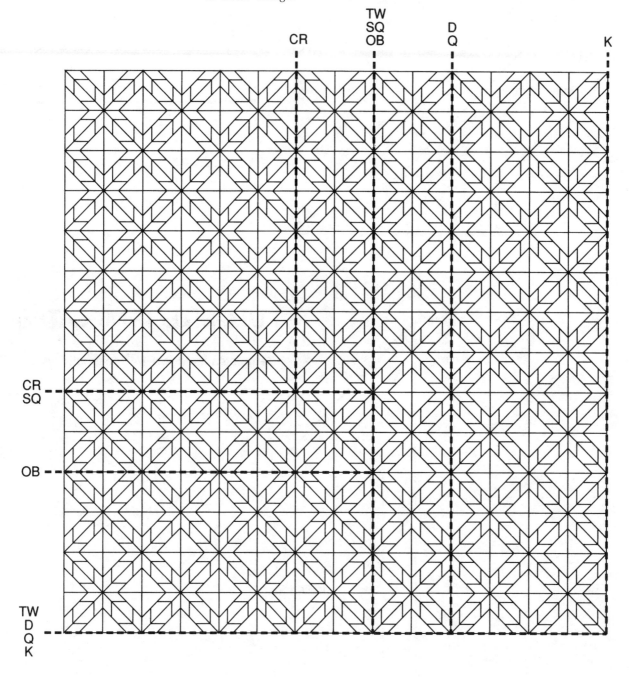

16. AUNT SUKEY'S CHOICE
INTERMEDIATE

To Speed-Cut:

A. Square

B. Long Diamond, 45°

C. Triangle, 45°

Lattice Strip, Rectangle

Lattice Squares, Square

Cutting Notes: The B pieces are mirror images. Stack fabric with "like" sides together.

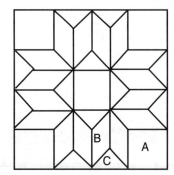

Piecing

A. Piecing the Block:

Step 1. Sew B units as shown (Fig. 1). Press to light side.

Fig. 1

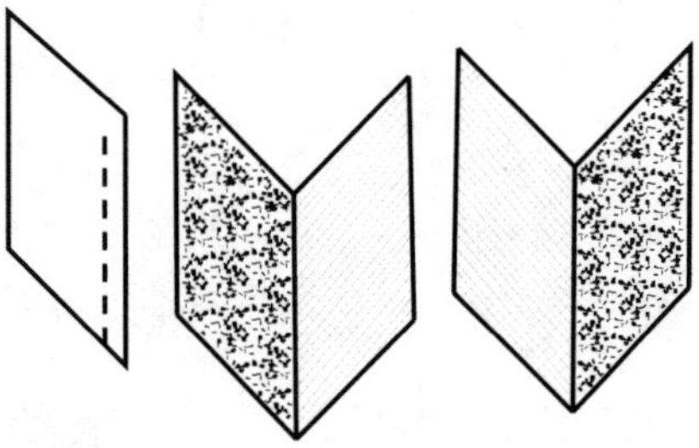

Step 2. Add background C piece to each B unit (Fig. 2).

Step 3. Join B units (Fig. 3).

Fig. 2

Fig. 3

Step 4. Add background A (Fig. 4).

Step 5. Sew center Cs to center A (Fig. 5). Press to Cs.

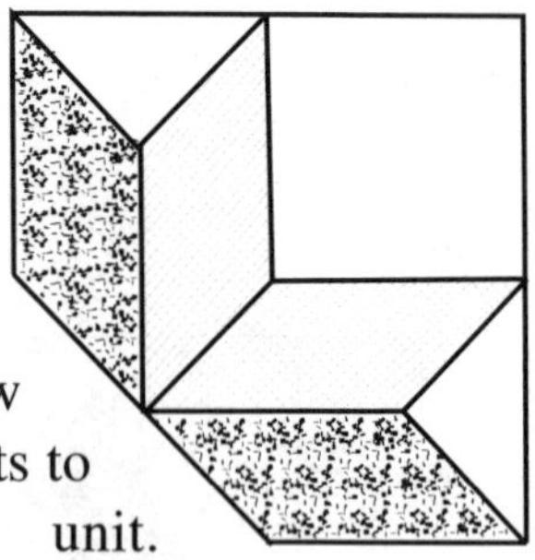

Step 6. Sew corner units to center unit. (Fig. 6). Press to center.

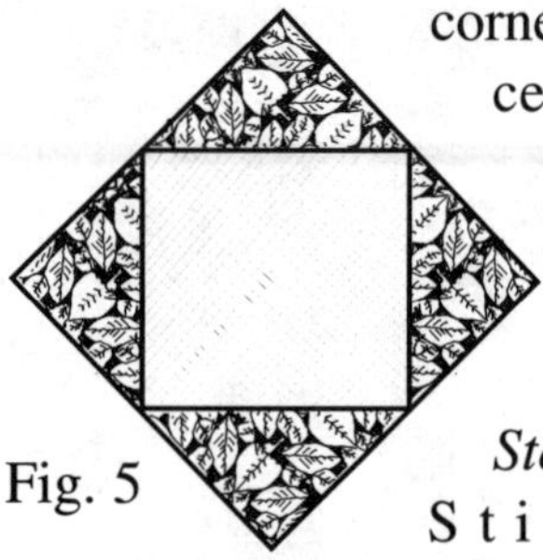

Fig. 4

Fig. 5

Step 7. Stitch remaining B seams.

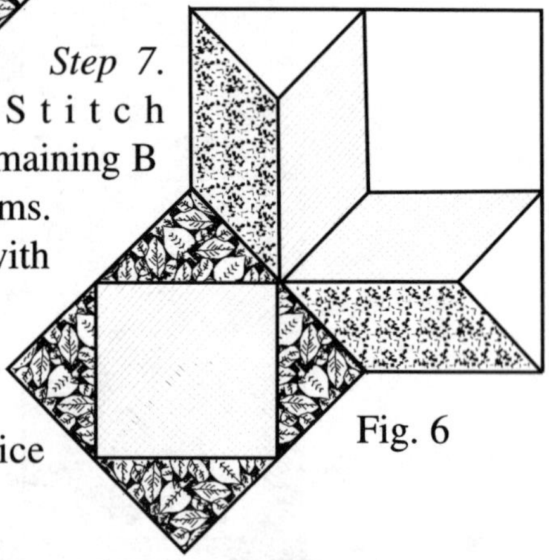

B. Join blocks with lattice strips and blocks:

Step 1. Sew blocks to lattice strips (Fig. 7).

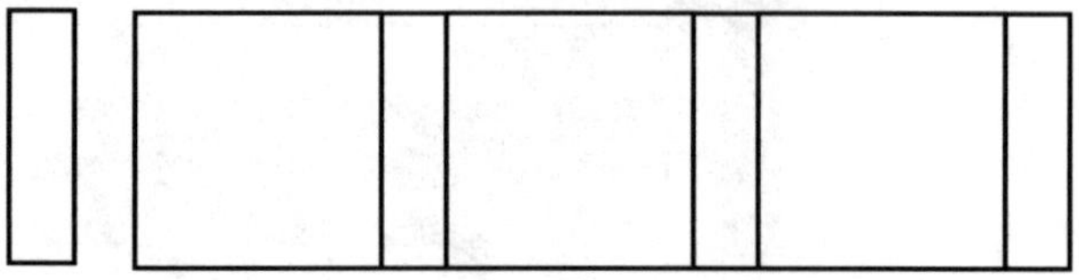

Fig. 6

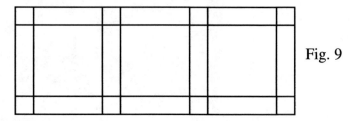

Fig. 7

Step 2. Sew lattice corners to lattice strips (Fig. 8).

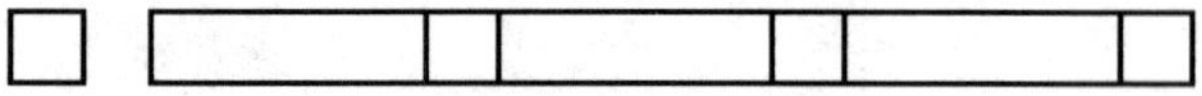

Fig. 8

Step 3. Join blocks to strips (Fig. 9).

Fig. 9

C. Add borders

Finishing

A. Quilt as desired.

B. Bind edges.

DIMENSIONS (INCHES)

	CR	TW	D	Q	K	SQ	OB
Finished Quilt	52x66	74x103	88x103	91x105	107x107	62x62	58x72
Center	46x60	60x89	74x89	75x89	89x89	46x46	46x60
Border 1	4-1/2	2	2	2	2	2	2
Border 2	-	5	5	6	7	6	4

CUTTING INSTRUCTIONS

	CR	TW	D	Q	K	SQ	OB
A - (Center Square)	12	24	30	30	36	9	12
A - (Background)	48	96	120	120	144	36	48
B - Fabric 1 & 2 (each)	96	192	240	240	288	72	96
C - (Background)	96	192	240	240	288	72	96
C - (Center Triangles)	48	96	120	120	144	36	48
Lattice Strips cut 3x12-1/2	31	58	71	71	84	24	31
Lattice Squares cut 3x3	20	35	42	42	49	16	20
Cut Widths Border 1	6″	2-1/2″	2-1/2″	2-1/2″	2-1/2″	2-1/2″	2-1/2″
Border 2	-	6-1/2″	6-1/2″	7-1/2″	8-1/2″	7-1/2″	5-1/2″

For additional information on cutting borders, see page 73.

GENERAL INFORMATION

	CR	TW	D	Q	K	SQ	OB
Blocks Across	3	4	5	5	6	3	3
Blocks Down	4	6	6	6	6	3	4
Total	12	24	30	30	36	9	12

YARDAGES

	CR	TW	D	Q	K	SQ	OB
A - (Center Square)	1/4	3/8	3/8	3/8	1/2	1/4	1/4
A - (Background)	5/8	1-1/8	1-1/4	1-1/4	1-5/8	1/2	5/8
B - Fabric 1 & 2 (each)	3/4	1-1/2	1-3/4	1-3/4	2	5/8	3/4
C - (Background)	1/2	7/8	1	1	1-1/2	3/8	1/2
C - (Center Triangles)	1/4	1/2	5/8	5/8	3/4	1/4	1/4
Lattice Strips	1-1/8	1-7/8	2-1/4	2-1/4	2-1/2	3/4	1-1/8
Lattice Squares	1/4	3/8	1/2	1/2	1/2	1/4	1/4
Border 1	3/4	3/4	7/8	7/8	1	1/2	1/2
Border 2	-	1-5/8	1-7/8	2-1/4	2-3/4	1-1/4	1
Backing	3-1/4	6-3/4	8-1/4	8-1/2	10-1/4	4	3-3/4

For additional information on yardages, see page 73.

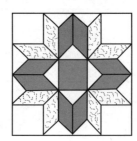

FULL-SIZE TEMPLATES

Templates include a 1/4" seam allowance

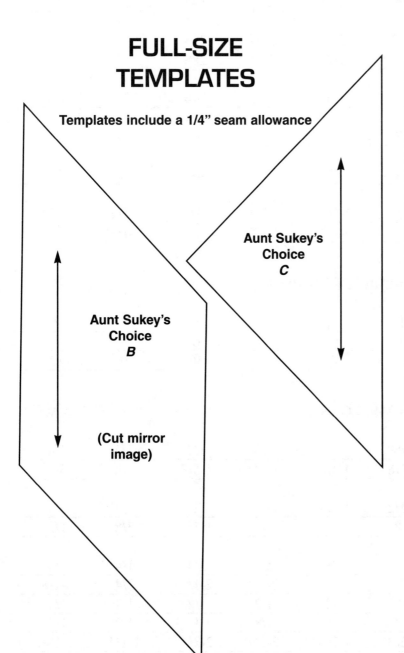

Aunt Sukey's Choice
C

Aunt Sukey's Choice
B

(Cut mirror image)

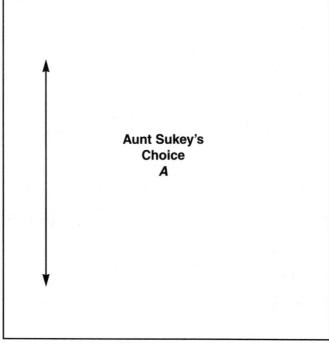

Aunt Sukey's Choice
A

AUNT SUKEY'S CHOICE
DESIGN PAGE

For a quick reference or design-your-own:
1. Copy this page.
2. Trim copy to desired quilt size.
3. Color design.

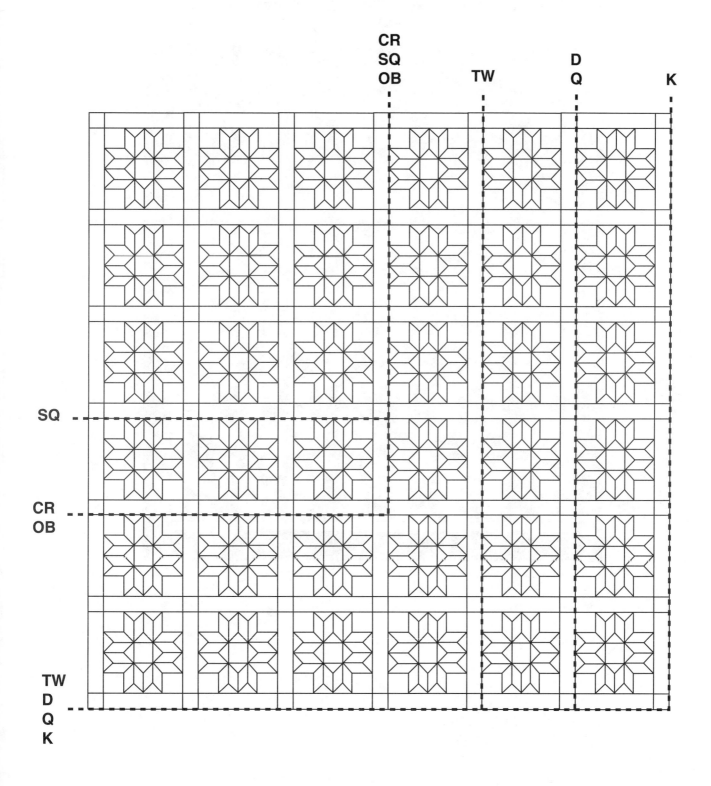

17. SIX-POINT STAR
INTERMEDIATE

To Speed-Cut:

A, B. Hexagon
C. Gemstone, 60°

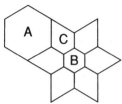

Piecing

NOTE: Hand-piecing the star units will be faster and easier than machine-piecing. You'll probably want to hand-piece the remainder of the quilt, too. If, however, speed is important, the longer seams may be machine-pieced very nicely.

A. Piecing basic units:
Step 1. Join star units (Fig. 1).
Step 2. Add large hexagons (Fig. 2).

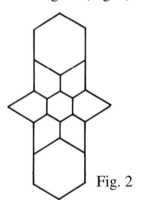

Fig. 1

Fig. 2

B. Joining units:
Step 1. Join as shown (Fig. 3).
Step 2. Trim edges even (Fig. 4).
C. Add borders.

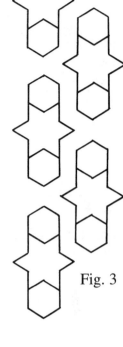

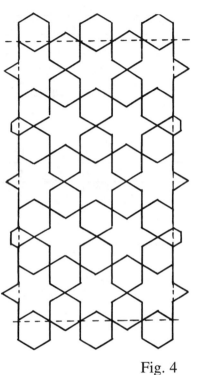

Fig. 3

Fig. 4

Finishing

A. Quilt as desired.
B. Bind edges.

DIMENSIONS (INCHES)

	CR	TW	D	Q	K	SQ	OB
Finished Quilt	44x58	69x104	86x104	90x108	107x108	62x65	58x72
Center	38x53	47x82	64x82	64x82	81x82	52x55	38x52
Border 1	3	1-1/2	1-1/2	1-1/2	1-1/2	1-1/2	1-1/2
Border 2	-	3	3	3	3	3	2-1/2
Border 3	-	6-1/2	6-1/2	8-1/2	8-1/2	-	6

CUTTING INSTRUCTIONS

	CR	TW	D	Q	K	SQ	OB
Number needed							
A - Fabric 1	72	132	180	180	228	104	72
B - Fabric 2	32	61	83	83	105	46	32
C - Fabric 3	198	376	508	508	640	282	198
Cut Widths							
Border 1	4-1/2″	2″	2″	2″	2″	2″	2″
Border 2	-	3-1/2″	3-1/2″	3-1/2″	3-1/2″	4-1/2″	3″
Border 3	-	8″	8″	10″	10″	-	7-1/2″

For additional information on cutting borders, see page 73.

GENERAL INFORMATION

	CR	TW	D	Q	K	SQ	OB
Units Across (Columns)	9	11	15	15	19	13	9
Stars Down	4	6	6	6	6	4	4
Total Units	32	61	83	83	105	46	32

YARDAGES

	CR	TW	D	Q	K	SQ	OB
Fabric 1 (A)	1-3/4	3	4	4	4-3/4	2-1/8	1-3/4
Fabric 2 (B)	3/8	5/8	7/8	7/8	1	1/2	3/8
Fabric 3 (C)	1-1/2	2-3/4	3-1/2	3-1/2	4-1/2	2	1-1/2
Border 1	3/4	3/4	3/4	3/4	3/4	3/4	1/2
Border 2	-	1	1-1/4	1-1/4	1-1/2	1	3/4
Border 3	-	2-1/2	2-1/2	3-1/4	3-3/4	-	1-3/4
Backing	2-3/4	6-1/4	8	8	1 0	3-3/4	3-1/2

For additional information on yardages, see page 73.

OPTIONS

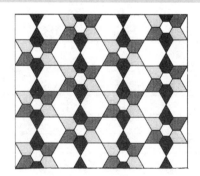
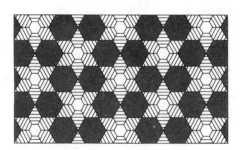
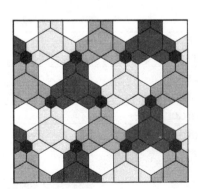

FULL-SIZE TEMPLATES

Templates include a 1/4" seam allowance

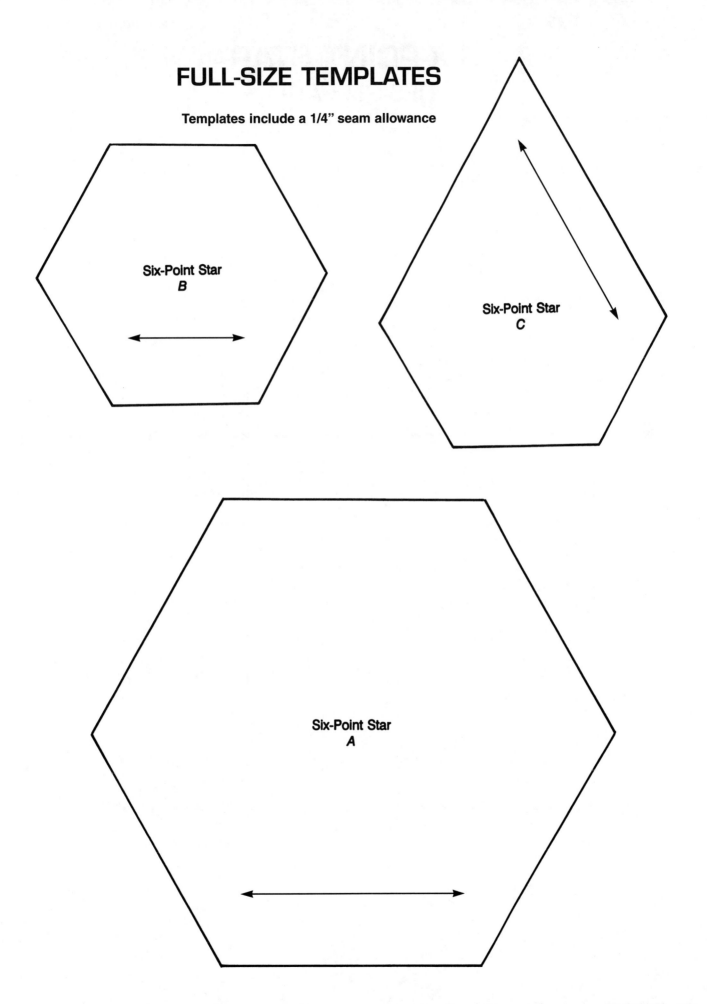

Six-Point Star
B

Six-Point Star
C

Six-Point Star
A

SIX-POINT STAR
DESIGN PAGE

For a quick reference or design-your-own:
1. Copy this page.
2. Trim copy to desired quilt size.
3. Color design.

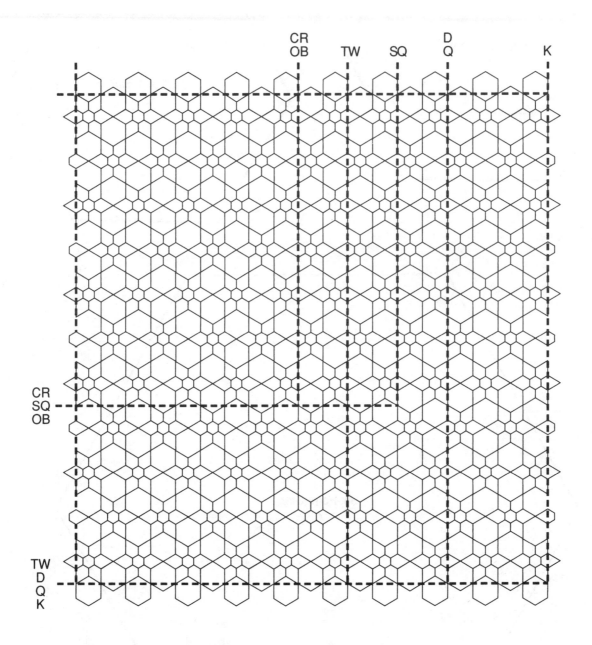

18. HUGS AND KISSES
ADVANCED

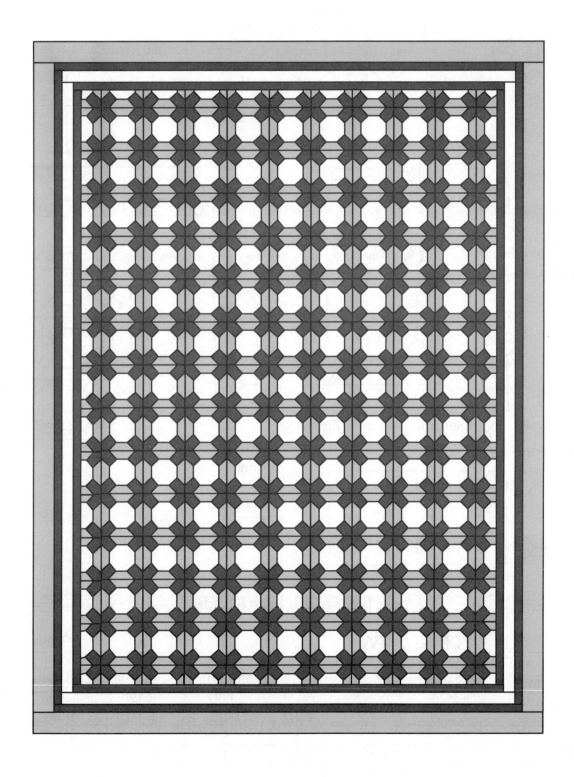

To Speed-Cut:
A. Octagon
B. Wedge, 45°
C, D. Candle, 45°

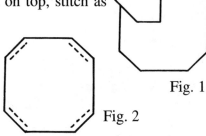

Piecing
A. Piecing basic units:

Step 1. Center C pieces on short sides of A piece (Fig. 1).

Step 2. With A on top, stitch as shown (Fig. 2).

Step 3. With A on top, inset B pieces on remaining sides (Fig. 3).

Step 4. Join B and C pieces (Fig. 4).

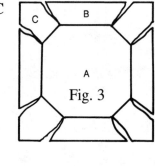

Fig. 1

Fig. 2

Fig. 3

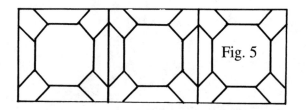

Fig. 4

Step 5. Join squares (Fig.5).

Fig. 5

B. Piecing outer rows:

NOTE: One outer row of "half-units" is added to complete the design and create a lovely, floating look.

Step 1. Cut A pieces in half, as needed, for edge pieces (Fig. 6). Cut one A piece in fourths for corners (Fig. 7).

Step 2. Join pieces as shown (Fig. 8).

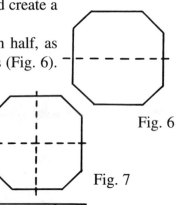

Fig. 6

Fig. 7

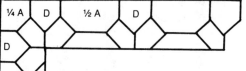

Step 3. Add outer rows to quilt (Fig. 9).

Fig. 8

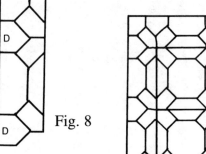

Fig. 9

C. Add borders.

Finishing
A. Quilt as desired.
B. Bind edges.

DIMENSIONS (INCHES)

	CR	TW	D	Q	K	SQ	OB
Finished Quilt	48x60	70x106	84x108	86x110	108x108	64x64	60x72
Center	42x54	59x95	72x96	73x97	96x96	56x56	54x66
Border 1	2	1-1/2	1-1/2	1-1/2	1-1/2	1-1/2	2
Border 2	4	3	3	4	3	2-1/2	4
Border 3	-	1-1/2	1-1/2	1-1/2	1-1/2	4	-
Border 4	-	5	6	6	6	-	-

CUTTING INSTRUCTIONS

	CR	TW	D	Q	K	SQ	OB
Number Needed							
A - Fabric 3	48	112	140	140	196	64	80
B - Fabric 2	164	404	512	512	728	221	284
C - Fabric 1	188	444	556	556	780	252	316
D - Fabric 3	28	44	48	48	56	36	36
Cut Widths							
Border 1	2-1/2″	2″	2″	2″	2″	2″	2-1/2″
Border 2	5-1/2″	3-1/2″	3-1/2″	4-1/2″	3-1/2″	3″	5-1/2″
Border 3	-	2″	2″	2″	2″	5-1/2″	-
Border 4	-	6-1/2″	7-1/2″	7-1/2″	7-1/2″	-	-

For additional information on cutting borders, see page 73.

GENERAL INFORMATION

	CR	TW	D	Q	K	SQ	OB
Blocks Across	5	7	9	9	13	7	7
Blacks Down	7	13	13	13	13	7	9
Total	35	91	117	117	169	49	63

YARDAGES

	CR	TW	D	Q	K	SQ	OB
Fabric 1 (C)	1	2	2-3/8	2-3/8	3-1/4	1-1/4	1-1/8
Fabric 2 (B)	1	2	2-1/2	2-1/2	1-1/4	1/2	5/8
Fabric 3 (A, D)	1-1/4	2-1/4	2-5/8	2-5/8	3 1/2	1-1/4	1-3/4
Border 1	3/4	3/4	3/4	3/4	3/4	3/4	3/4
Border 2	1-1/2	1	1-1/4	1-1/2	1-1/2	1	1-1/2
Border 3	-	3/4	3/4	3/4	3/4	1-1/2	-
Border 4	-	2	2-1/2	2-1/2	3	-	-
Backing	3-1/4	6-3/4	8-1/2	8-1/2	10-1/4	4	3-3/4

For additional information on yardages, see page 73.

OPTIONS

  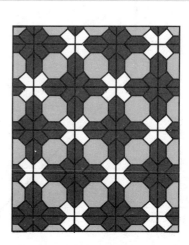

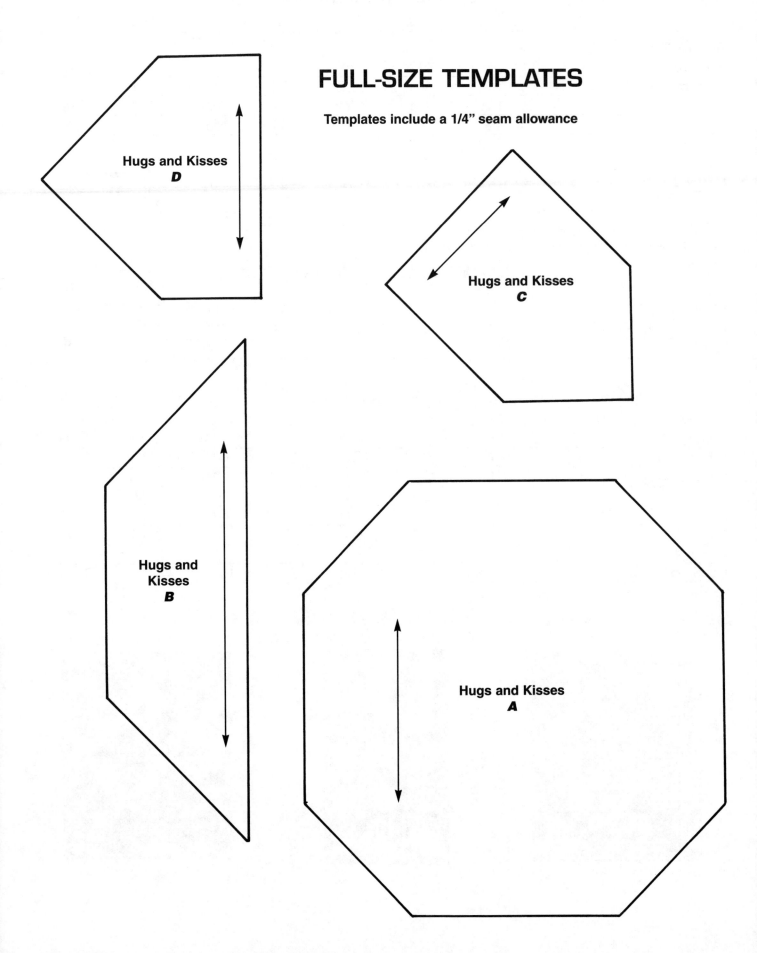

FULL-SIZE TEMPLATES

Templates include a 1/4" seam allowance

Hugs and Kisses
D

Hugs and Kisses
C

Hugs and
Kisses
B

Hugs and Kisses
A

HUGS AND KISSES
DESIGN PAGE

For a quick reference or design-your-own:
1. Copy this page.
2. Trim copy to desired quilt size.
3. Color design.

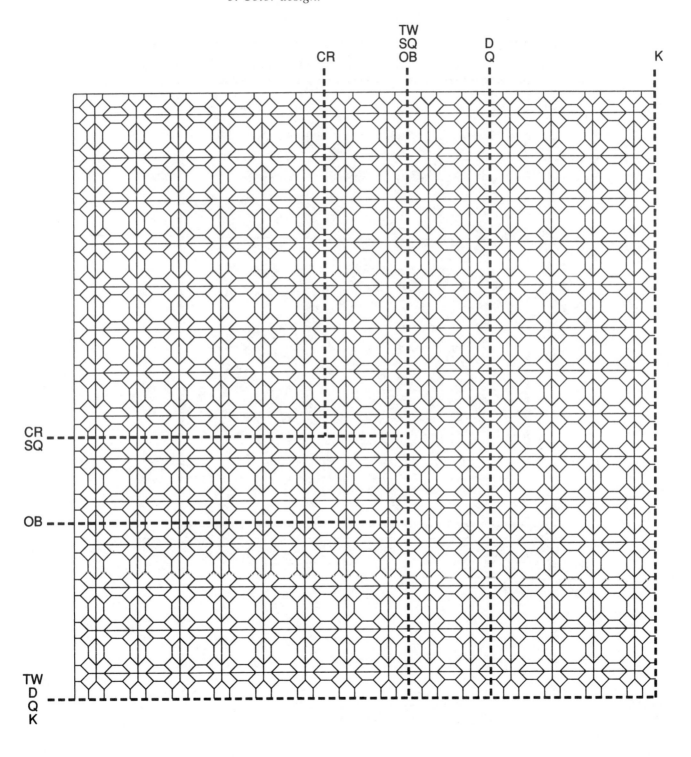

19. NOSEGAY
ADVANCED

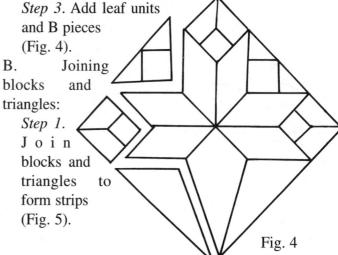

To Speed-Cut:

A, B. Odd-shape Triangle, 45°

C. Long Diamond, 45°

D, G. Square

E. Triangle, 45°

F. Shoe, 45°

Squares for Edge Triangles: Cut 14″ x 14″, cut in half, diagonally.

Squares for Corner Triangles: Cut 10-1/2″ x 10-1/2″, cut in half diagonally.

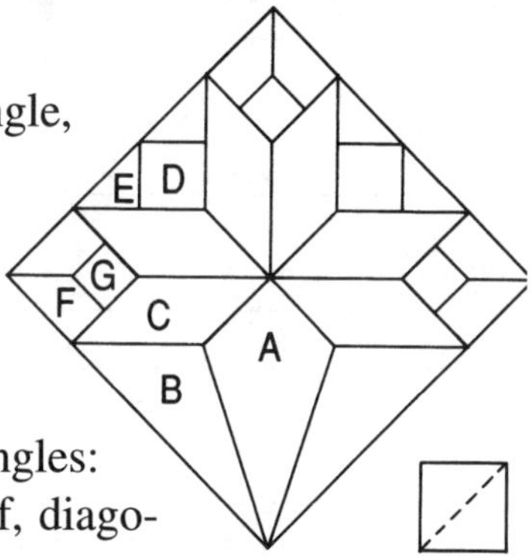

Cutting Notes: So many shapes in this block are mirror images that, just to be safe, stack all of the fabrics with like sides together.

Piecing

A. Piecing blocks:

Step 1. Piece leaf units (Fig. 1).

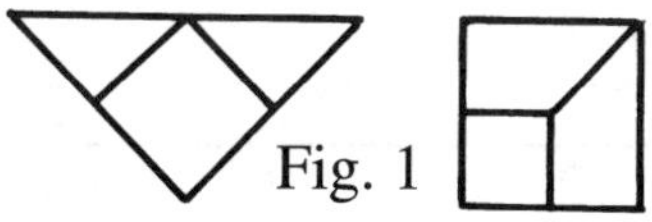

Step 2. Piece petal and cone units (Figs. 2 and 3).

Fig. 1

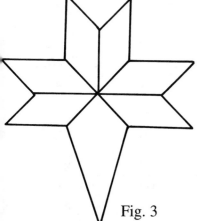

Fig. 3

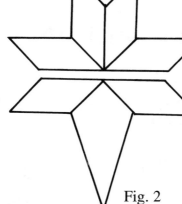

Fig. 2

Step 3. Add leaf units and B pieces (Fig. 4).

B. Joining blocks and triangles:

Step 1. Join blocks and triangles to form strips (Fig. 5).

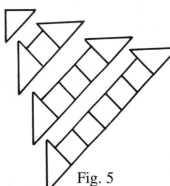

Fig. 4

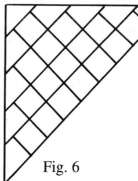

Fig. 5

Step 2. Join strips (Fig. 6).

C. Add borders.

Finishing

A. Quilt as desired.

B. Bind edges.

Fig. 6

DIMENSIONS (INCHES)

	CR	TW	D	Q	K	SQ	OB
Finished Quilt	47x64	70x104	87x104	91x108	110x110	66x66	58x75
Center	35x52	52x86	69x86	69x86	86x86	52x52	52x69
Border 1	2	1-1/2	1-1/2	1-1/2	1-1/2	2	3
Border 2	4	3	3	3	3	5	-
Border 3	-	4-1/2	4-1/2	1-1/2	1-1/2	-	-
Border 4	-	-	-	5	6	-	-

CUTTING INSTRUCTIONS

	CR	TW	D	Q	K	SQ	OB
Number needed							
A - Fabric 1	8	23	32	32	41	13	18
C - Fabric 2							
(Cut mirror image)	48	138	192	192	246	78	108
D - Fabric 3	16	46	64	64	82	26	36
G - Fabric 4	24	69	96	96	123	39	54
B - Fabric 5							
(Cut mirror image)	16	46	64	64	82	26	36
F - Fabric 5							
(Cut mirror image)	48	138	192	192	246	78	108
E - Fabric 5	32	92	128	128	164	52	72
Side Triangles							
Fabric 6	6	12	14	14	16	8	10
Corner Triangles							
Fabric 6	4	4	4	4	4	4	4
Cut Widths							
Border 1	2-1/2″	2″	2″	2″	2″	2-1/2″	4-1/2″
Border 2	5-1/2″	3-1/2″	3-1/2″	3-1/2″	3-1/2″	6-1/2″	-
Border 3	-	6″	6″	2″	2″	-	-
Border 4	-	-	-	6-1/2″	7-1/2″		-

For additional information on cutting borders, see page 73.

GENERAL INFORMATION

	CR	TW	D	Q	K	SQ	OB
Blocks Across	2	3	4	4	5	3	3
Blocks Down	3	5	5	5	5	3	4
Total	8	23	32	32	41	13	18

YARDAGES

	CR	TW	D	Q	K	SQ	OB
Fabric 1 (A)	3/8	3/4	1	1	1-1/4	1/2	5/8
Fabric 2 (C)	7/8	2-1/4	3-1/4	3-1/4	4	1-1/4	1-3/4
Fabric 3 (D)	1/2	3/8	1/2	1/2	1/2	1/4	3/8
Fabric 4 (G)	1/8	1/4	3/8	3/8	1/2	1/4	1/4
Fabric 5 (B, E, F)	1	2	2-3/4	2-3/4	3-3/8	1-3/8	1-3/4
Fabric 6 (Triangles)	1	1-1/2	1-3/4	1-3/4	1-3/4	1	1-1/2
Border 1	3/4	3/4	3/4	3/4	3/4	3/4	1-1/4
Border 2	1-1/2	1	1-1/4	1-1/4	1-1/2	1-3/4	-
Border 3	-	1-3/4	2	3/4	3/4	-	-
Border 4	-	-	-	2-1/4	3	-	-
Backing	3	6-1/4	8	8	10-1/4	4	3-1/2

For additional information on yardages, see page 73.

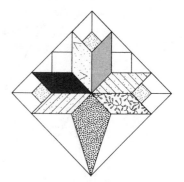

FULL-SIZE TEMPLATES

Templates include a 1/4" seam allowance

Cut squares for:
Edges: 14 x 14
Corners: 10-1/2 x 10-1/2

Cut diagonally to make triangles

Nosegay
A

Nosegay
E

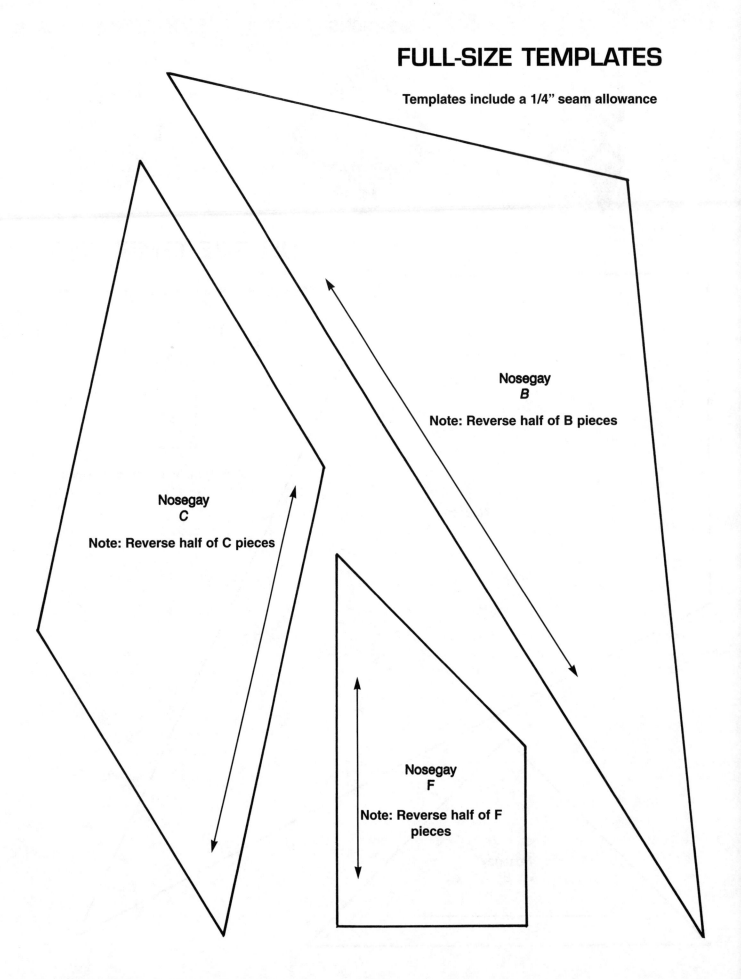

FULL-SIZE TEMPLATES

Templates include a 1/4" seam allowance

Nosegay
B

Note: Reverse half of B pieces

Nosegay
C

Note: Reverse half of C pieces

Nosegay
F

**Note: Reverse half of F
pieces**

FULL-SIZE TEMPLATES

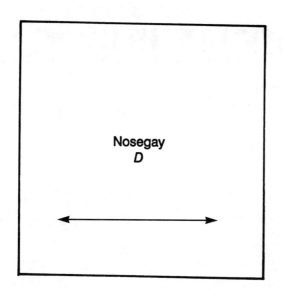

Nosegay
D

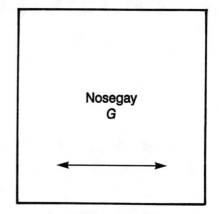

Nosegay
G

**Templates include a
1/4" seam allowance**

NOSEGAY
DESIGN PAGE

For a quick reference or design-your-own:
1. Copy this page.
2. Trim copy to desired quilt size.
3. Color design.

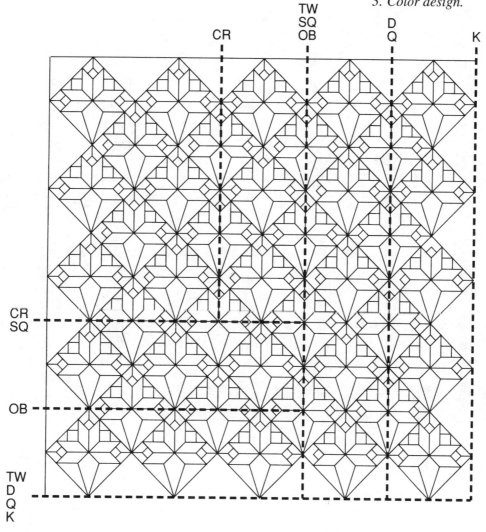

20. DOUBLE WEDDING RING
ADVANCED

To Speed-Cut:
B. Crescent
C, E. Arc Pieces
D. Square

Cutting Notes: Cut crescents and centers (A) as shown (Fig. 1). Stack fabric right side up for E pieces on left end of arc and wrong side up for those on the right end of arc (Fig. 2).

Piecing
A. Piecing units:

Step 1. Sew arc pieces as shown (short arcs) (Fig. 3).

Step 2. Add corner squares to both ends of half the arc units (long arcs) (Fig. 4).

Step 3. Pin short arc to crescent piece at center point (Fig. 5). With crescent on top, stitch to pin (Fig. 6). With needle in fabric, match ends of seam. Stitch remainder of seam (Fig. 7).

Step 4. Pin long arc to crescent/arc unit. Pin at center point and corner seams (Fig. 8). Stitch as in Step 3 (Fig. 9).

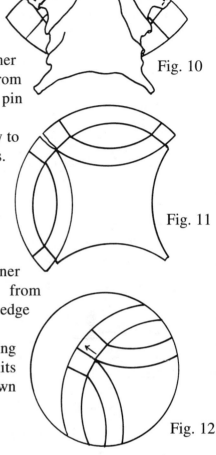

Single arc

Fig. 1

E—Right End
Right :
E—Left End
Fig. 2

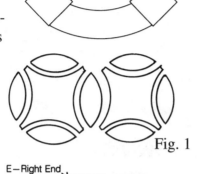

Fig. 3
Press

Fig. 4

Fig. 5

Fig. 6

Fig. 7

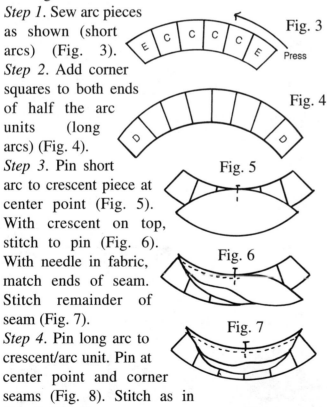

Fig. 8

Fig. 9

B. Joining the units:

Step 1. Pin center piece to crescent unit. Pin at center point and corner seams. Working from the center out, pin remainder of seam. (Fig. 10). Stitch only to these corner seams. Backstitch lightly.

Step 2. Join crescent unit to adjacent side of center piece (Fig. 11).

Step 3. Join corner blocks, stitching from inner ring to outer edge (Fig. 12).

Step 4. Join remaining crescents/center units to form rows as shown in layout (Fig. 13).

Step 5. Join rows (Fig. 14).

Fig. 10

Fig. 11

Fig. 12

Fig. 13

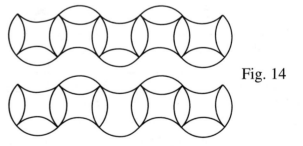

Fig. 14

Finishing
A. Quilt as desired.
B. Cut bias binding 2-1/4″ wide. Bind, following curved edges.

DIMENSIONS (INCHES)

	CR	TW	D	Q	K	SQ	OB
Finished Quilt	41x63	74x96	86x96	86x108	108x108	63x63	63x74

CUTTING INSTRUCTIONS

	CR	TW	D	Q	K	SQ	OB
A - Fabric 1	15	48	56	63	81	25	30
B - Fabric 1	38	110	127	142	180	60	71
C - Fabric 2-5 (each)	76	220	254	284	360	120	142
E - Fabric 6-7 (each)	76	220	254	284	360	120	142
D - Fabric 8-9 (each)	48	126	144	160	200	72	84
Binding	Cut bias strip 2-1/4″ wide						
Single Arc*	76	220	254	284	360	120	142

*Optional (replaces C&E pieces)

GENERAL INFORMATION

	CR	TW	D	Q	K	SQ	OB
Rings Across	3	6	7	7	9	5	5
Rings Down	5	8	8	9	9	5	6
Total	15	48	56	63	81	25	30

YARDAGES

	CR	TW	D	Q	K	SQ	OB
Fabric 1 (A, B)	2-1/4	5-1/4	6-1/4	6-3/4	8-1/2	3-1/4	4
Fabric 2-5 (C) (each)	3/4	1-1/2	1-1/2	1-3/4	2-1/2	7/8	1
Fabric 6 & 7 (E) (each)	3/4	1-1/2	1-1/2	1-3/4	2-1/2	7/8	1
Fabric 8 & 9 (D) (each)	3/8	3/4	7/8	7/8	1-1/2	1/2	5/8
Backing	2	6	6-3/4	7-3/4	10-1/2	4	4
Binding	2-1/8	3-1/8	3-1/4	3-1/2	5	2-3/8	2-1/2
Single Arc*	2-1/4	5-1/2	6-3/8	7-1/8	9	3-1/2	3-7/8

*Optional (replaces C & E pieces)

For additional information on yardages, see page 73.

OPTIONS

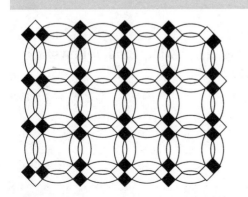
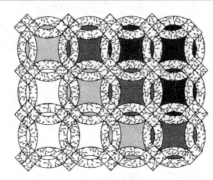
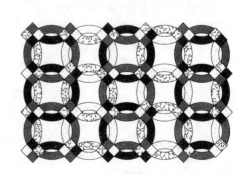

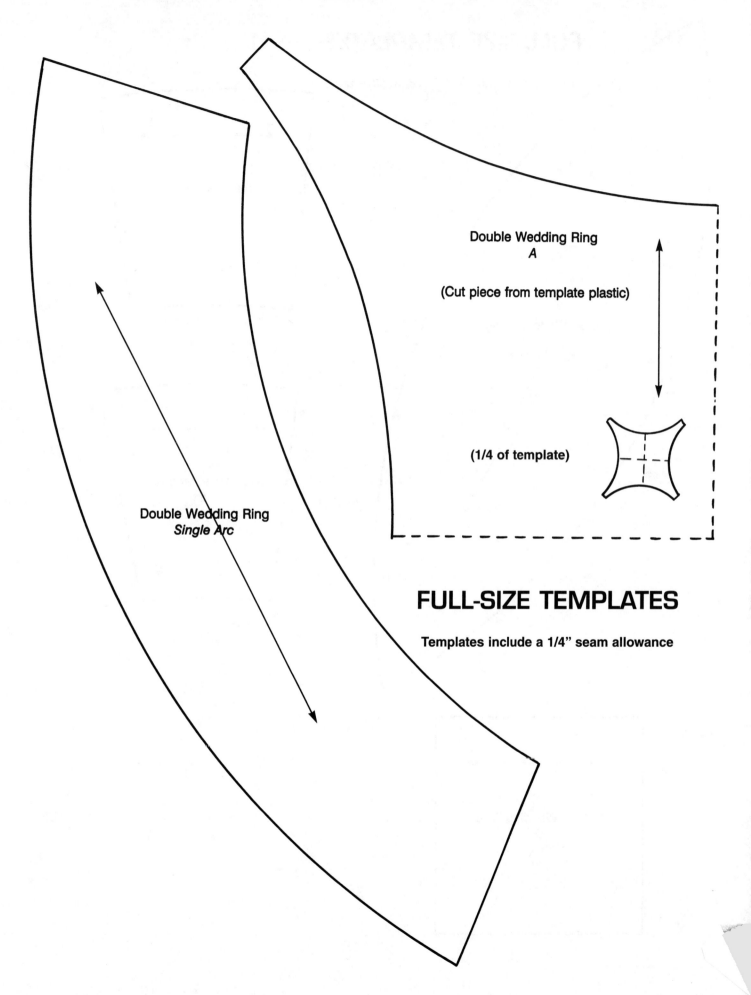

Double Wedding Ring
A

(Cut piece from template plastic)

(1/4 of template)

Double Wedding Ring
Single Arc

FULL-SIZE TEMPLATES

Templates include a 1/4" seam allowance

FULL-SIZE TEMPLATES

Templates include a 1/4" seam allowance

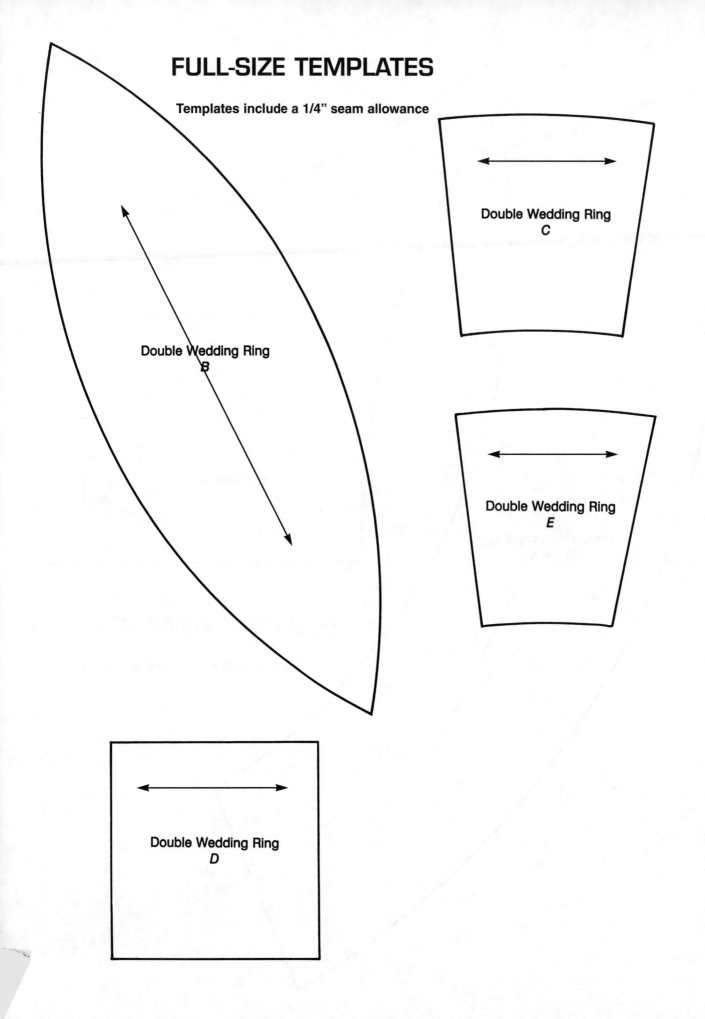

Double Wedding Ring
C

Double Wedding Ring
B

Double Wedding Ring
E

Double Wedding Ring
D

DOUBLE WEDDING RING
DESIGN PAGE

For a quick reference or design-your-own:
1. Copy this page.
2. Trim copy to desired quilt size.
3. Color design.

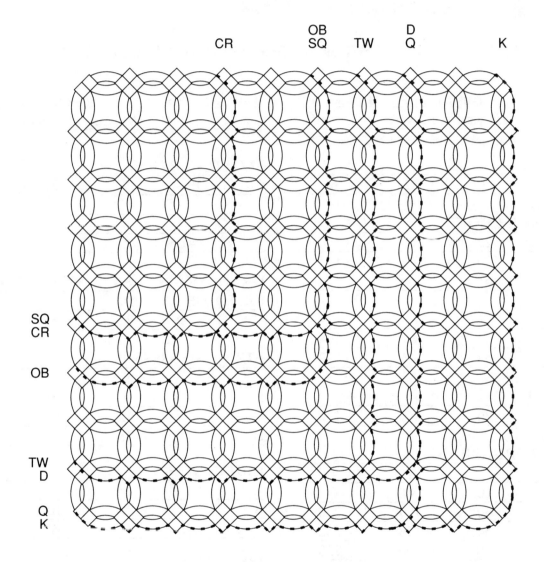

Now that you've learned my Speedy System, you can apply the knowledge to all of your quilts! No longer will you look at a gorgeous quilt pattern and think, "I'd love to make that, but the thought of drawing around all of those little pieces is just too depressing. Forget it." Now you'll grab my book, thumb through it until you find the methods for each of those pieces, and merrily dive right in!

A YARDAGE CHARTS, BORDERS, AND BACKING

YARDAGE CHART FOR TEMPLATES FOR DESIGN-YOUR-OWN USE

TEMPLATE	NUMBER OF PIECES FROM:		
	1/4 yard	1/2 yard	1 yard
ALWAYS FRIENDS			
A	8	32	64
AUNT SUKEY'S CHOICE			
A	22	44	99
B	36	72	153
C	68	136	272
BOW TIE			
A	24	48	108
B	54	126	252
CLAMSHELL			
A	26	52	130
DOUBLE WEDDING RING			
A	-	4	12
B	10	30	60
C	40	100	220
D	54	126	252
E	40	100	220
Single Arc	8	20	44
DRESDEN PLATE			
A	12	36	72
B	24	48	108
FAN			
A	16	32	64
B	24	48	120

TEMPLATE	NUMBER OF PIECES FROM:		
	1/4 yard	1/2 yard	1 yard
FLOATING STARS			
CR, SQ, OB - A	7	21	49
- B	46	115	253
T, D, Q, K - A	6	18	36
- B	42	105	231
GRANDMOTHER'S FLOWER GARDEN			
CR, SQ, OB - A	39	78	169
T, D, Q, K - A	22	55	121
HUGS AND KISSES			
A	9	27	63
B	50	100	220
C	42	112	224
D	48	96	192
INDIAN STAR			
A	16	48	96
B	39	104	208
C	30	80	160
LOVE RING			
CR, SQ, OB - A	24	48	108
- B	48	96	192
T, D, Q - A	9	27	63
- B	26	65	143
K - A	7	14	35
- B	22	44	99

TEMPLATE	NUMBER OF PIECES FROM:		
	1/4 yard	1/2 yard	1 yard

MAGNOLIAS

A	9	27	63
B	28	70	154
C	48	96	192
D	80	160	352
E	140	280	588

NINE-PATCH CHAIN

Small Square	80	160	340
Large Square	8	24	48

NOSEGAY

A	6	18	36
B	12	24	48
C	14	35	77
D	32	80	176
E	48	112	224
F	26	104	208
G	63	168	336

TEMPLATE	NUMBER OF PIECES FROM:		
	1/4 yard	1/2 yard	1 yard

PINEY WOODS

A	30	60	130
B	75	150	325

SIX-POINT STAR

A	7	21	42
B	24	60	132
C	24	60	132

TUMBLING BLOCKS

A	42	84	182
B	30	70	140
C	52	117	234

TEXAS TRELLIS

A	30	60	130
B	75	150	325

WINDMILL

A	20	50	100

BORDERS

Measurements include finished widths, from the quilt edge to the finished edge.

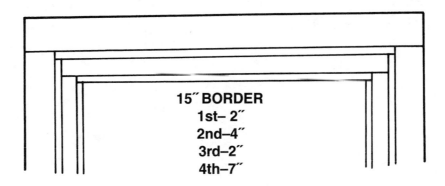

15″ BORDER
1st– 2″
2nd–4″
3rd–2″
4th–7″

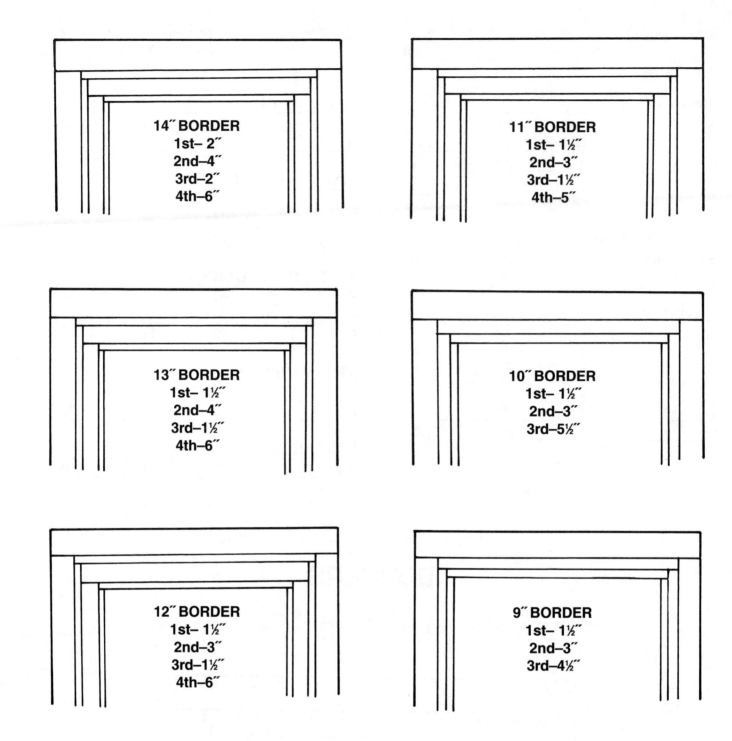

14″ BORDER
1st– 2″
2nd–4″
3rd–2″
4th–6″

11″ BORDER
1st– 1½″
2nd–3″
3rd–1½″
4th–5″

13″ BORDER
1st– 1½″
2nd–4″
3rd–1½″
4th–6″

10″ BORDER
1st– 1½″
2nd–3″
3rd–5½″

12″ BORDER
1st– 1½″
2nd–3″
3rd–1½″
4th–6″

9″ BORDER
1st– 1½″
2nd–3″
3rd–4½″

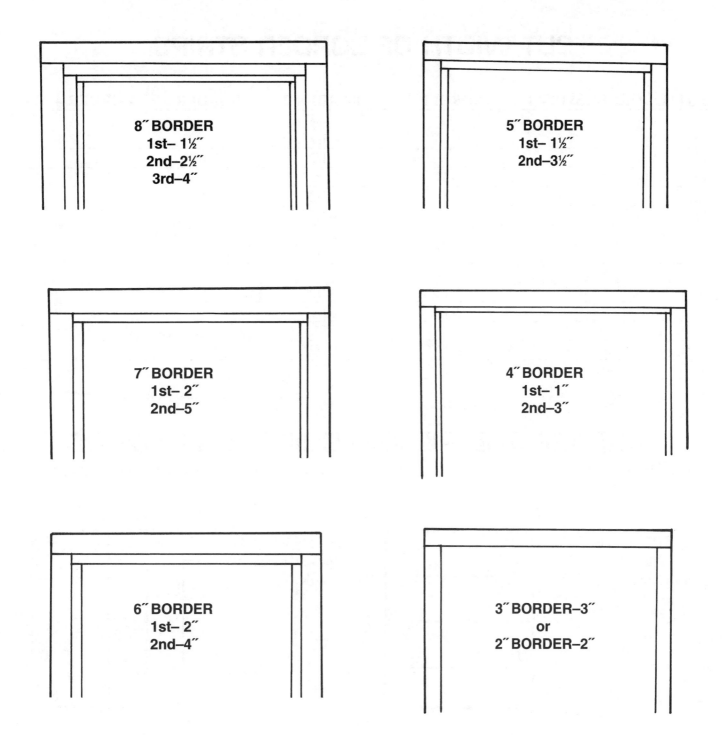

8″ BORDER
1st– 1½″
2nd–2½″
3rd–4″

5″ BORDER
1st– 1½″
2nd–3½″

7″ BORDER
1st– 2″
2nd–5″

4″ BORDER
1st– 1″
2nd–3″

6″ BORDER
1st– 2″
2nd–4″

3″ BORDER–3″
or
2″ BORDER–2″

CUT WIDTH OF BORDER STRIPS

TOTAL BORDER WIDTH	BORDER 1	BORDER 2	BORDER 3	BORDER 4
15″	2-1/2″	4-1/2″	2-1/2″	8-1/2″
14″	2-1/2″	4-1/2″	2-1/2″	7-1/2″
13″	2″	4-1/2″	2″	7-1/2″
12″	2″	3-1/2″	2″	7-1/2″
11″	2″	3-1/2″	2″	6-1/2″
10″	2″	3-1/2″	7″	
9″	2″	3-1/2″	6″	
8″	2″	3″	5-1/2″	
7″	2-1/2″	6-1/2″		
6″	2-1/2″	5-1/2″		
5″	2″	5″		
4″	1-1/2″	4-1/2″		
3″	4-1/2″			
2″	3-1/2″			

YARDAGE AND PIECING GUIDE FOR BACKING

Yardage includes a small amount of shrinkage and waste. The arrows indicate the lengthwise grain of the fabric.

Crib: 3-1/4 yards.
Oblong tablecloth:
3-3/4 yards

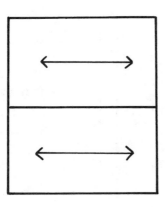

Twin: 6-3/4 yards
Square tablecloth:
4 yards

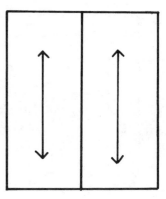

Double:
8-1/2 yards
Queen:
8-1/2 yards

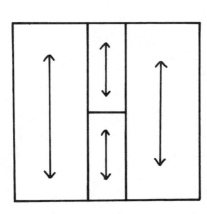

King:
10-1/4 yards

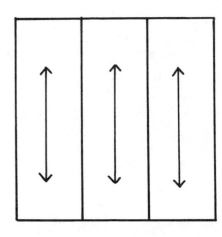

APPENDIX

B 30 BASIC SHAPES TO SPEED-CUT

The following are instructions for speed-cutting 30 shapes. Most shapes are used in at least one of the quilts featured later in this book.

For each of these 30 shapes, I name the template you will need (for example, square or 60° diamond). You may have many of these templates on hand. Others (such as the Drunkard's Path) can be found with the quilts they are used in (see the 20 Quilts section). The Miterite is an 8″ x 24″ ruler with one end cut off at a 45° angle. As you will see by studying the optional templates listed for each shape, this basic template can be used to cut the major portion of your quilt pieces.

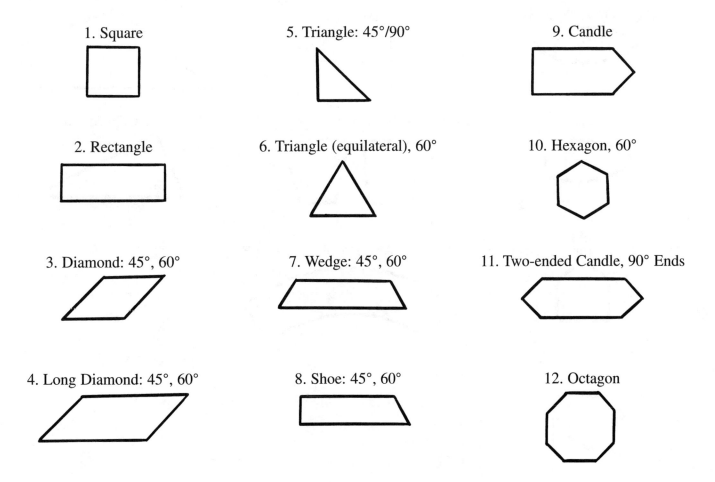

1. Square

2. Rectangle

3. Diamond: 45°, 60°

4. Long Diamond: 45°, 60°

5. Triangle: 45°/90°

6. Triangle (equilateral), 60°

7. Wedge: 45°, 60°

8. Shoe: 45°, 60°

9. Candle

10. Hexagon, 60°

11. Two-ended Candle, 90° Ends

12. Octagon

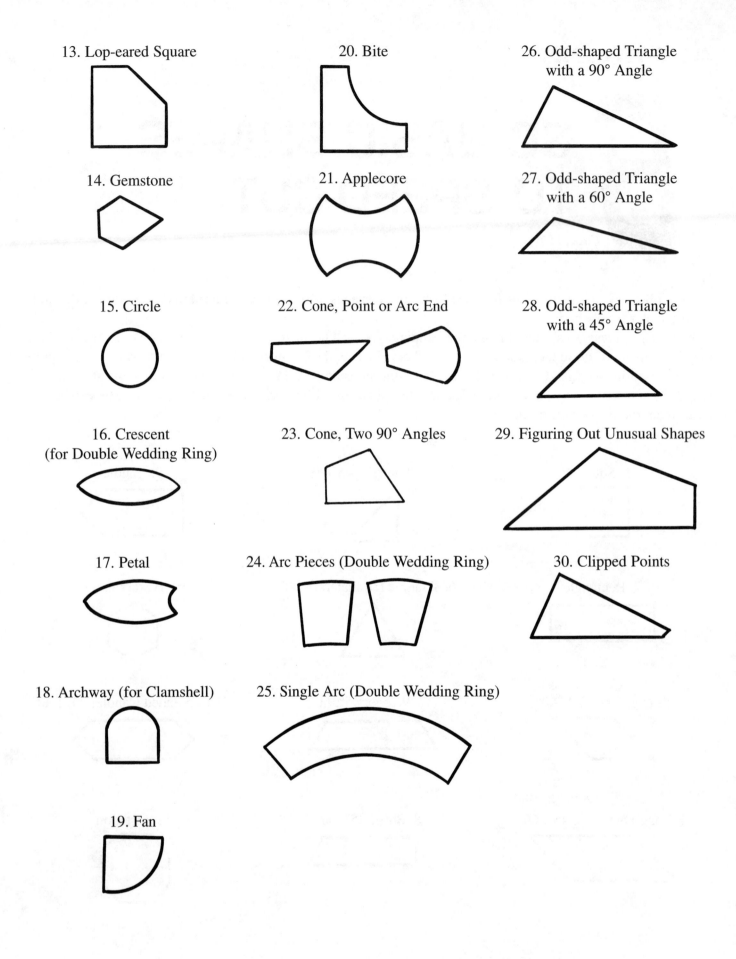

13. Lop-eared Square

14. Gemstone

15. Circle

16. Crescent
(for Double Wedding Ring)

17. Petal

18. Archway (for Clamshell)

19. Fan

20. Bite

21. Applecore

22. Cone, Point or Arc End

23. Cone, Two 90° Angles

24. Arc Pieces (Double Wedding Ring)

25. Single Arc (Double Wedding Ring)

26. Odd-shaped Triangle
with a 90° Angle

27. Odd-shaped Triangle
with a 60° Angle

28. Odd-shaped Triangle
with a 45° Angle

29. Figuring Out Unusual Shapes

30. Clipped Points

1. SQUARE

Basic Shape

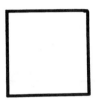

Variations

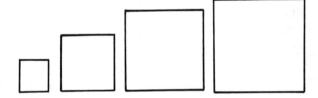

Basic Strip

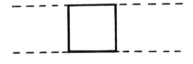

Taping and Using Basic Template (Square)

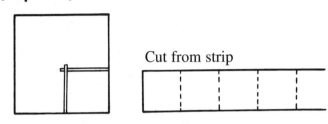

Cut from strip

Optional Templates

90° corner
45°/90° triangle
Basic ruler
Miterite

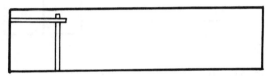

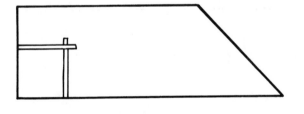

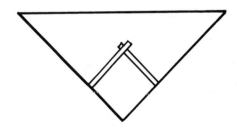

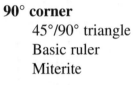

2. SQUARE

Basic Shape

Variations

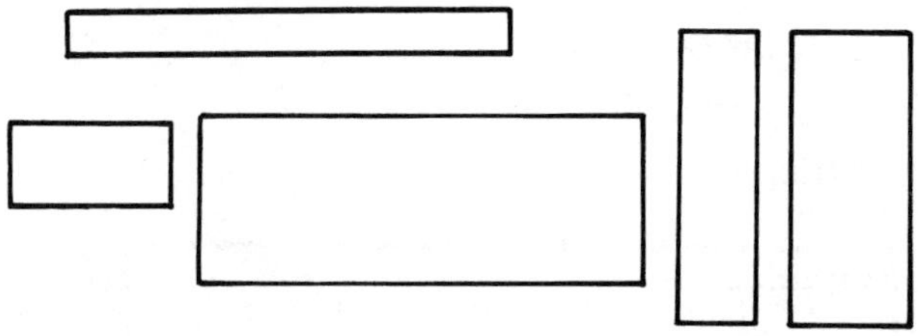

Basic Strip

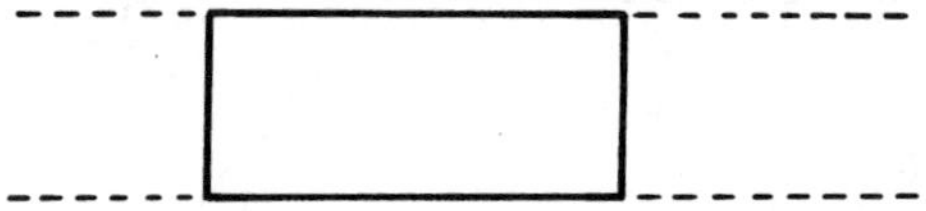

Taping and Using Basic Template (Square)

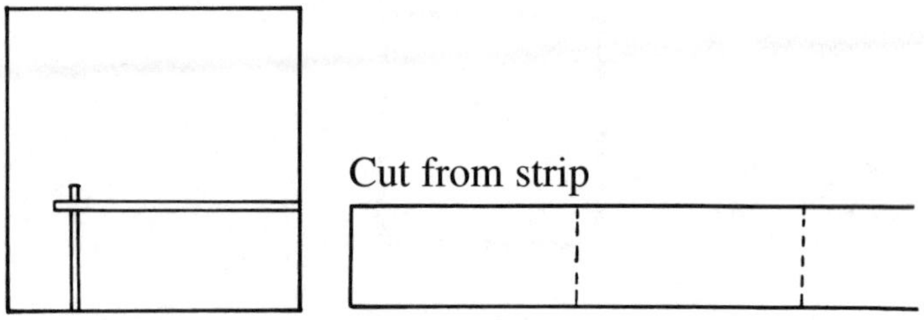

Cut from strip

Optional Templates

90° corner
    Basic ruler
    Miterite
    45°/90° triangle

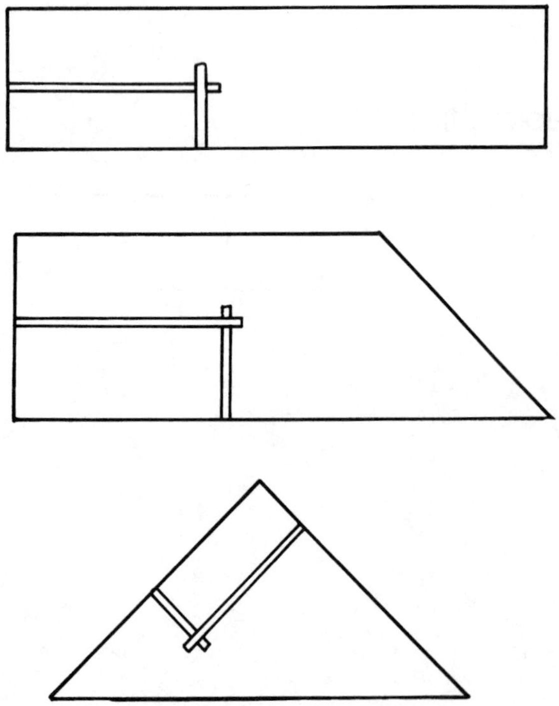

3. DIAMOND: 45°, 60°

Basic Shape

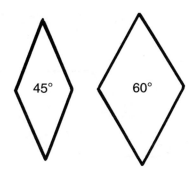

Variations

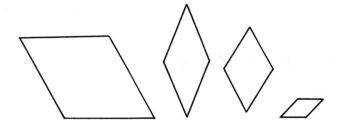

Basic Strip

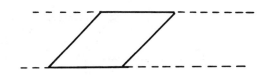

Taping and Using Basic Template (Diamond)

45° or 60°
Template

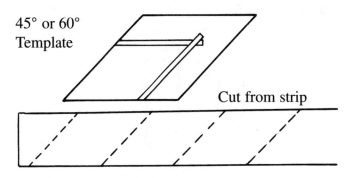

Cut from strip

Optional Templates

45° angle
Miterite
45° triangle
60° angle
60° triangle

45°

45°

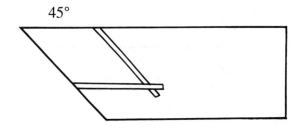

60°

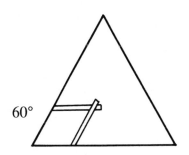

4. LONG DIAMOND: 45°, 60°

Basic Shape

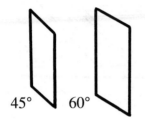

45°   60°

Variations

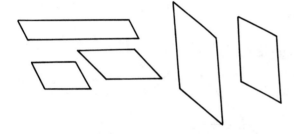

Basic Strip

Taping and Using Basic Template (Diamond)

45° or 60°
Template

Cut from strip

Optional Templates

45° angle
Miterite
45° triangle
60° angle
60° triangle

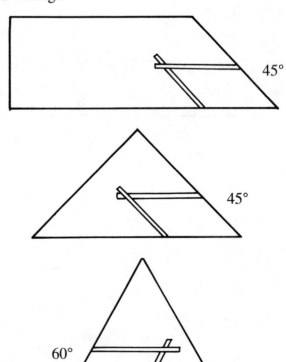

45°

45°

60°

5. TRIANGLE: 45°/90°

Basic Shape

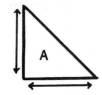

A Straight grain on short sides

B Straight grain on long side

Variations

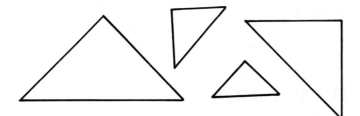

Basic Strip

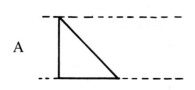

A

B

Taping and Using Basic Template (45° Triangle)

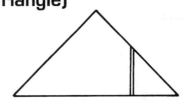

Cut from strip

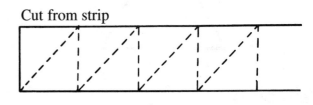

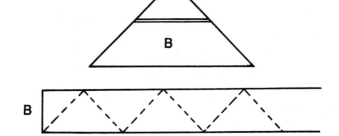

B

B

Optional Templates

45° corners
   Miterite
   45° diamond
   Squares, cut in half
   (makes two per square)
90° corners
   Miterite
   Square

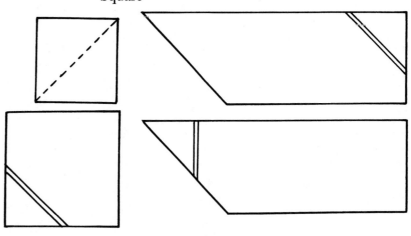

6. TRIANGLE (EQUILATERAL), 60°

Basic Shape

Variations

Basic Strip

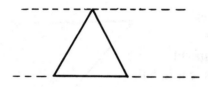

Taping and Using Basic Template (60° triangle)

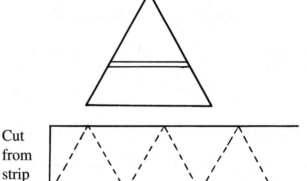

Cut from strip

Optional Templates

60° diamond

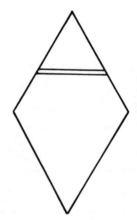

7. WEDGE: 45°, 60°

Basic Shape

Variations

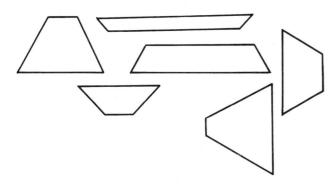

Basic Strip

Taping and Using Basic Template (45° or 60° triangle)

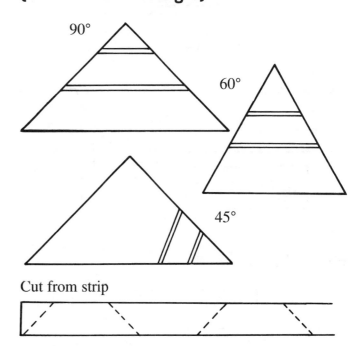

90°

60°

45°

Cut from strip

Optional Templates

90°, 60°, or 45° angles, as needed
   Miterite (90° or 45°)
   Diamonds (60° and 45°)
   Square (90°)

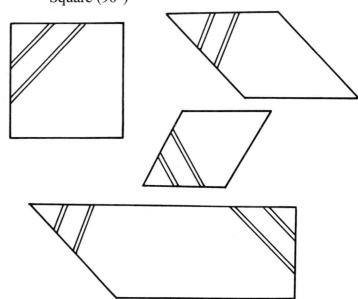

8. SHOE: 45°, 60°

Basic Shape

Variations

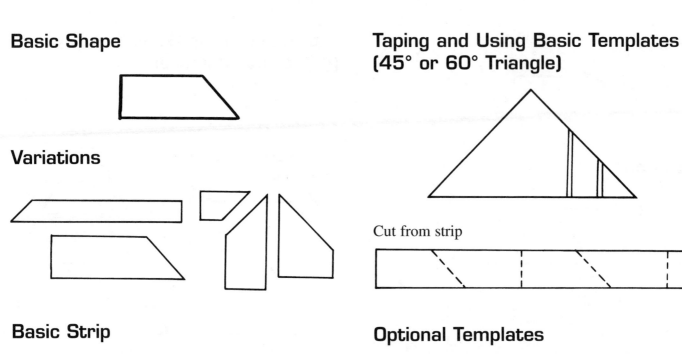

Basic Strip

Taping and Using Basic Templates
(45° or 60° Triangle)

Cut from strip

Optional Templates

45° angle
  Miterite
  45° diamond
60° angle
  60° diamond

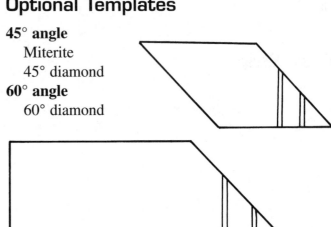

9. CANDLE

Basic Shape

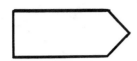

Variations

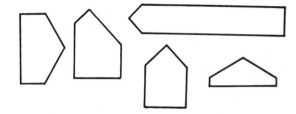

Basic Strip

Taping and Using Basic Template (45° Triangle)

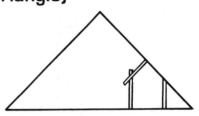

Cut from strip

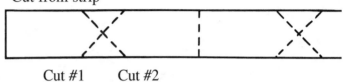

Cut #1   Cut #2

Optional Templates

45° angle
   Miterite

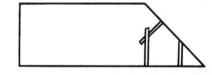

Hexagon
Square
Diamond

Use to cut end

PLUS

Use to cut corner, as needed

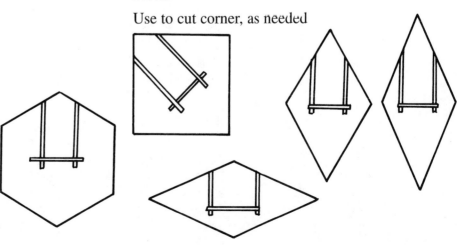

10. HEXAGON

Basic Shape

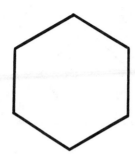

Variations

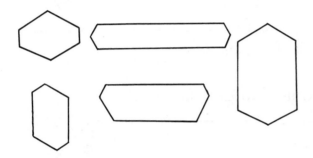

Basic Strip

Taping and Using Basic Template (Hexagon)

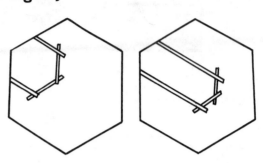

Cut from strip

Optional Templates

60° diamond
60° triangle

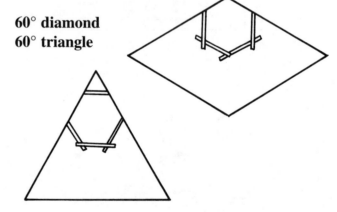

11. TWO-ENDED CANDLE, 90° ENDS

Basic Shape

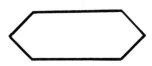

Variations

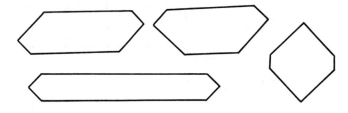

Basic Strip

Taping and Using Basic Template (45° Triangle)

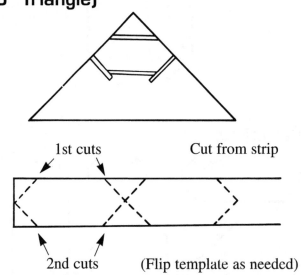

1st cuts · Cut from strip

2nd cuts · (Flip template as needed)

Optional Templates

90° angles
  Square
  Basic ruler
  Miterite

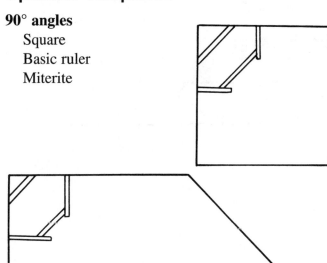

12. OCTAGON

Basic Shape

Variations

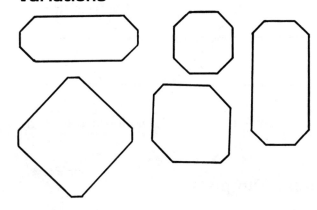

Basic Strip

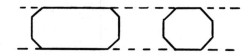

Taping and Using Basic Template (60° triangle)

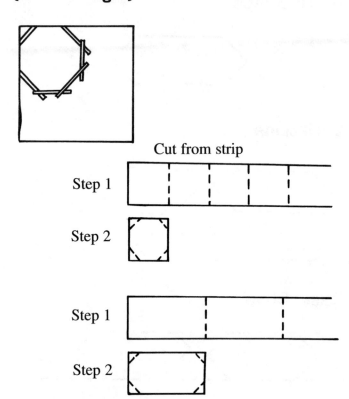

Cut from strip

Step 1

Step 2

Step 1

Step 2

Optional Templates

90° angle
45°/90° angle
Basic ruler
Miterite

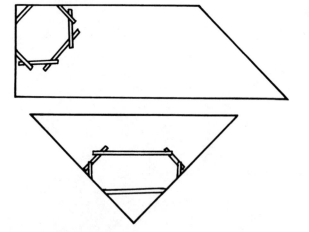

13. LOP-EARED SQUARE

Basic Shape

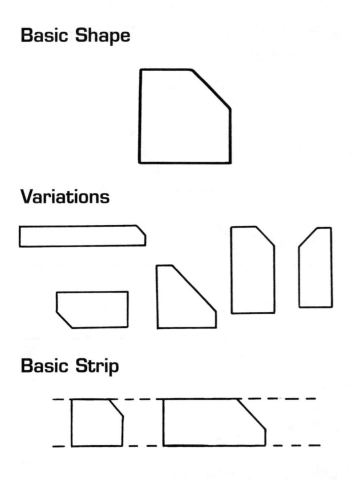

Variations

Basic Strip

Taping and Using Basic Template
(45° Triangle)

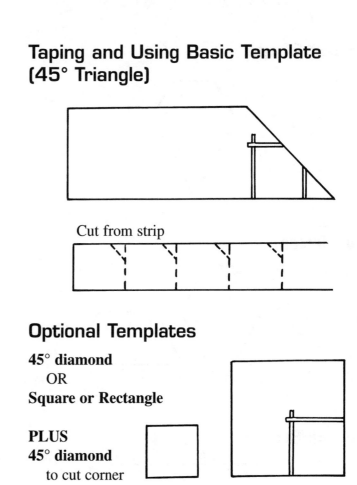

Cut from strip

Optional Templates

45° diamond
  OR
Square or Rectangle

PLUS
45° diamond
  to cut corner

14. GEMSTONE

Basic Shape

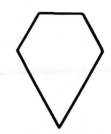

Variations

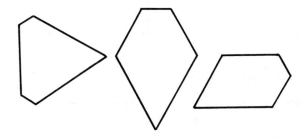

Basic Strip

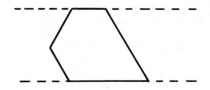

Taping and Using Basic Template (60° Diamond)

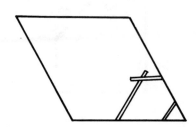

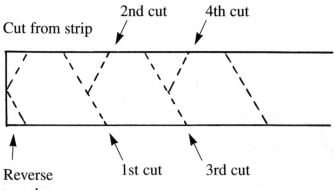

Cut from strip

2nd cut   4th cut

1st cut   3rd cut

Reverse template to cut off corner

Optional Templates

60° triangle

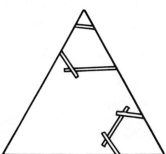

15. CIRCLE

Basic Shape

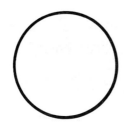

Basic Strip

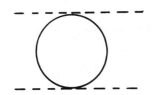

Using Basic Template (Circle, no taping needed)

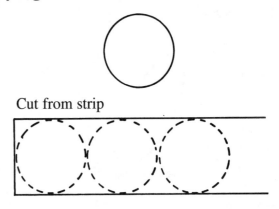

Cut from strip

Options

Cut circles from heavy template plastic. Cut no more than four layers of fabric at one time. Work carefully because the cutter will easily the plastic template.

Notes

Most circular pieces are appliquéd, so seam allowances may be larger than 1/4″. Use the next larger size circle than the pattern. The cardboard pressing template will determine the final shape. (See Chapter 5)

Cutting around circles on multiple layers is not as neat as cutting straight lines. With a little practice, though, you will soon become quite comfortable with it.

16. CRESCENT
(for Double Wedding Ring)

Basic Shape

Taping and Using Basic Template (Double Wedding Ring)

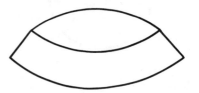

Cut from strip

Variations

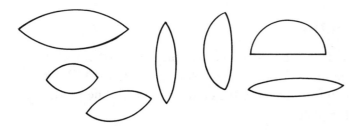

Optional Templates

Circle
Drunkard's Path

Note: Cut shapes do not have to be exact if the piece is to be appliquéd. The final shape will be determined by the pressing template. (See section on appliqué in Chapter 5)

Basic Strip

Cutting Procedure for Double Wedding Ring, no taping needed

If crescent is used for Double Wedding Ring, cut as shown to make best use of the fabric.

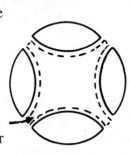

Use to cut ring center

17. PETAL

Basic Shape

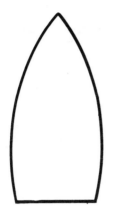

Variations

Basic Strip

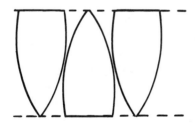

Taping and Using Basic Template (Double Wedding Ring)

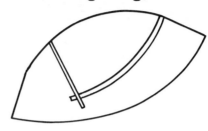

Cut from strip

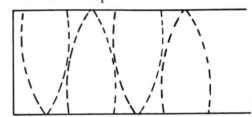

Optional Templates

Circle
Drunkard's Path

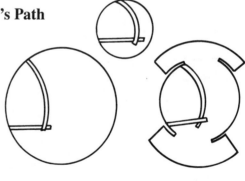

Use optional templates to vary base of petal

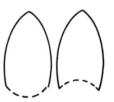

Note: Cut shapes do not have to be exact if the piece is to be appliquéd. The final shape will be determined by the pressing template. (See section on appliqué in Chapter 5)

18. ARCHWAY
(for Clamshell)

Basic Shape

Variations

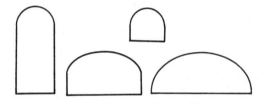

Basic Strip

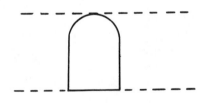

Taping and Using Basic Template (Circle)

Bottom need not be taped. Line up top of circle with top of rectangle.

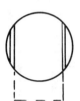

Cut from strip

Step 1

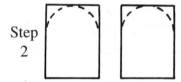

Step 2

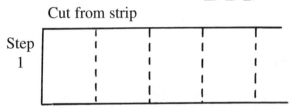

Optional Templates

Double Wedding Ring
Drunkard's Path
Circle

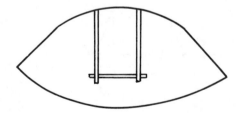

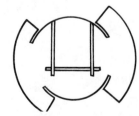
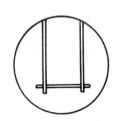

Note: Cut shapes do not have to be exact if the piece is to be appliquéd. The final shape will be determined by the pressing template. (See section on appliqué in Chapter 5)

19. FAN

Basic Shape

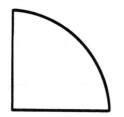

Variations

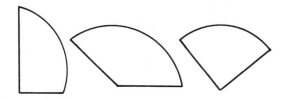

Basic Strip

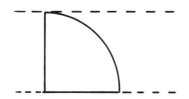

Taping and Using Basic Template
(Drunkard's Path)

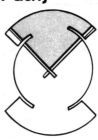

Cut from strip

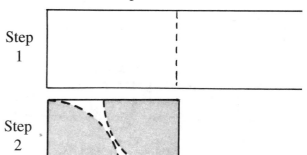

Step 1

Step 2

Optional Templates

90° corner
    Square
    Basic ruler
    Miterite

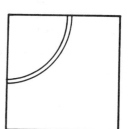

PLUS
Arc
    Double Wedding Ring
    Circle

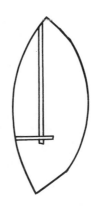

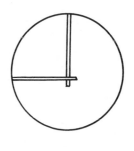

20. BITE

Basic Shape

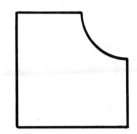

Variations

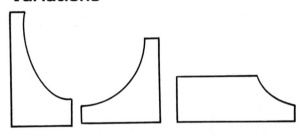

Basic Strip

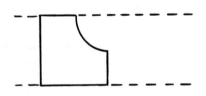

Taping and Using Basic Template (Drunkard's Path)

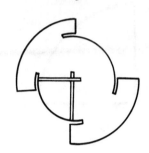

Cut from strip

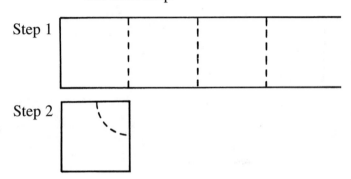

Step 1

Step 2

Optional Templates

Circle
Double Wedding Ring

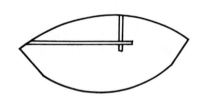

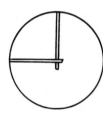

21. APPLECORE

Basic Shape

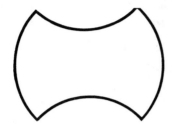

Variations

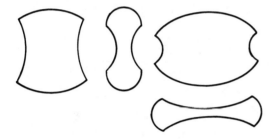

Basic Strip

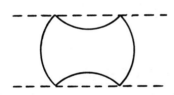

Taping and Using Basic Template (Circle)

Use in Step 1

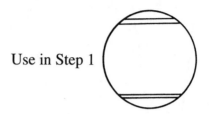

Cut from strip

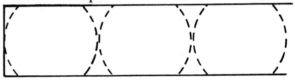

Use in Step 2

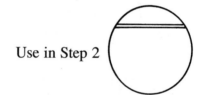

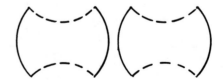

Optional Templates

Drunkard's Path
Double Wedding Ring

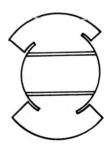

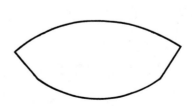

22. CONE, POINTED OR ARC END

Basic Shape

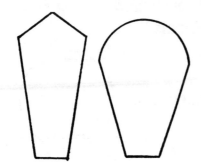

Variations

Basic Strip

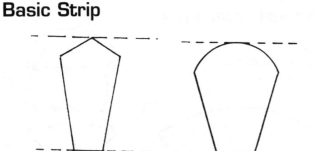

Taping and Using Basic Template (Circle and Square)

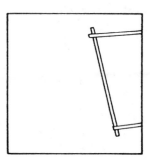

Cut from strip

Step 1

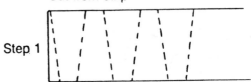

Use in Step 2

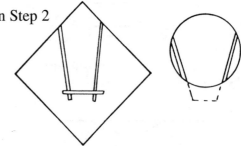

Optional Templates

Basic ruler
Miterite
Square

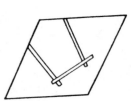

PLUS

Square, diamond, or triangle as needed for top pointed shape

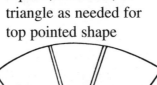

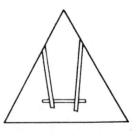

Drunkard's Path, Circle, or Double Wedding Ring as needed for top arc shape

Note: Shape of arc does not have to be exact if the piece is to be appliquéd. Final shape will be determined by the pressing template. (See section on appliqué in Chapter 5)

23. CONE, TWO 90° ANGLES

Basic Shape

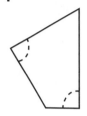

Variations

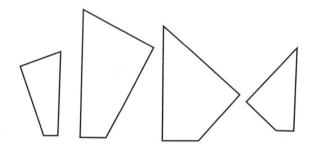

Basic Strip

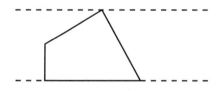

Taping and Using Basic Template (Square)

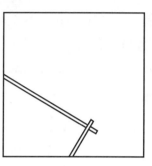

Step 1
Cut rectangles from strip

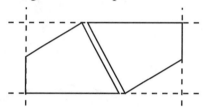

Step 2
Cut from rectangles

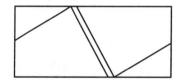

Optional Templates

Basic ruler
Miterite

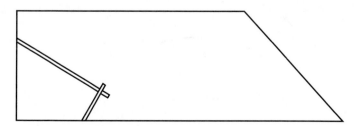

24. ARC PIECES
(for Double Wedding Ring)

Basic Shape

Variations

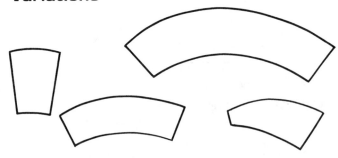

Using Basic Template (Double Wedding Ring, no taping needed)

Step1
    Cut arc

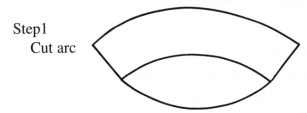

Step 2
    Cut pieces as needed

(piece C)

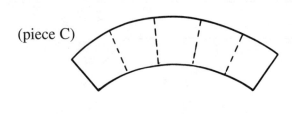

(piece E)

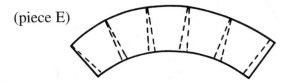

Basic Strip for Variations

Optional Templates for Variations

Basic ruler
Miterite
Square

PLUS
    Drunkard's Path, circles, or any template
    needed for top and bottom shapes

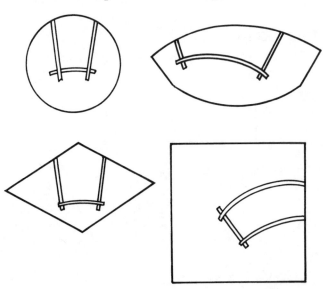

Note: The shape of the arc does not have to be
exact if the piece is to be appliquéd. Final shape
will be determined by the pressing template. (See
section on appliqué in Chapter 5)

25. SINGLE ARC
(for Double Wedding Ring)

Basic Shape

Variations

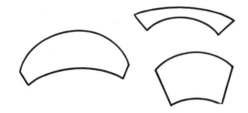

Using Basic Template (Double Wedding Ring, no taping needed)

Step 1
Cut arc

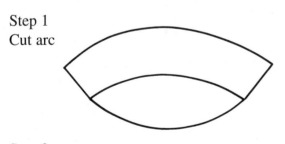

Step 2
Trim 1/4″ from both ends

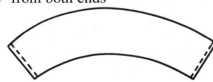

Basic Strip for Variations

Optional Templates for Variations

Basic ruler
Miterite
Square

PLUS

Circles, Drunkard's Path, or any template needed for top and bottom shapes

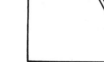

(Bottom shape)

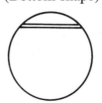

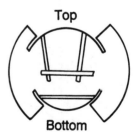

Top

Bottom

26. ODD-SHAPED TRIANGLE WITH A 90° ANGLE

Basic Shape

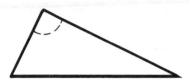

Variations

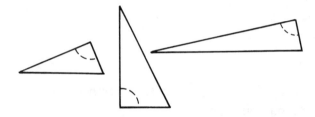

Basic Strip

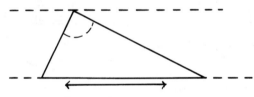

Straight grain on long edge

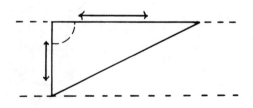

Straight grain on two shorter edges

Taping and Using Basic Template (Basic Ruler)

Option 1: If you want the straight grain on the long edge of the shape

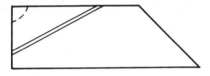

Cut from strip

Option 2: If you want the straight grain on the two shorter edges of the shape

Step 1

Step 2

Optional Templates
90° angle
    Miterite
    Square
    45° triangle

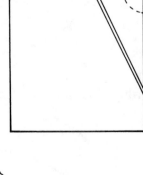

27. ODD-SHAPED TRIANGLE WITH A 60° ANGLE

Basic Shape

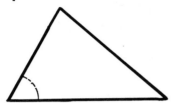

Variations

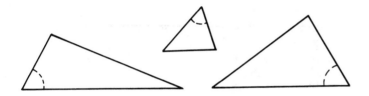

Basic Strip

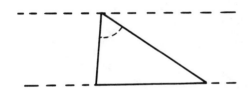

Taping and Using Basic Template (60° Triangle)

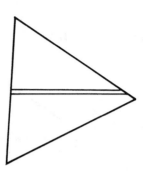

Cut from strip

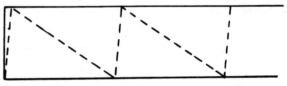

Optional Templates

60° Diamond

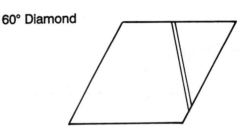

Note: The straight grain will be on the edge opposite of the 60° angle. To place the straight grain on any other edge, refer to Shape #29 (Figuring Out Unusual Shapes).

28. ODD-SHAPED TRIANGLE WITH A 45° ANGLE

Basic Shape

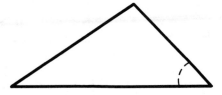

Variations

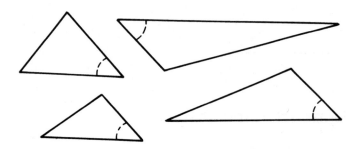

Basic Strip

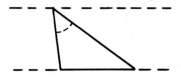

Taping and Using Basic Template (Miterite)

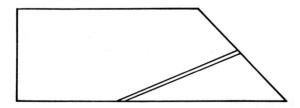

Cut from strip

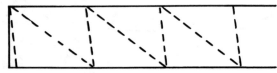

Optional Templates

45° triangle
45° diamond

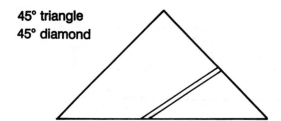

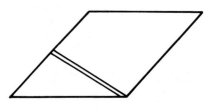

Note: The straight grain will be on the edge opposite of the 45° angle. To place the straight grain on any other edge, refer to Shape #29 (Figuring Out Unusual Shapes).

29. FIGURING OUT UNUSUAL SHAPES

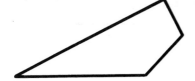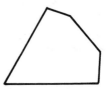

Occasionally you'll want to cut a piece that simply does not match any template available. The good news is that it still can be rotary-cut with your templates. Here's how:

Look for any angle that matches an angle of your templates. This will give you two cutting edges. If no angle can be found, then any piece with straight edges can be rotary-cut, one side at a time. Just follow this procedure:

One cut can be made by cutting a strip (this will be the straight grain of the piece).

Now place the template over the pattern and tape the template along as many straight edges as needed to cut the other sides of the shape.

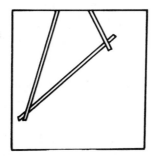

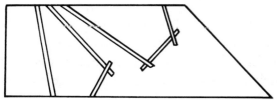

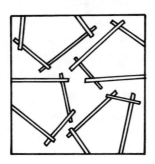

Cut pieces from the strips. Example of cutting sequence

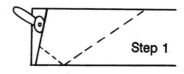
Step 1

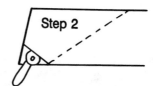
Step 2

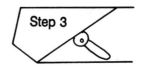
Step 3

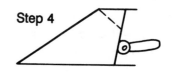
Step 4

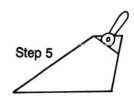
Step 5

Did you figure this one out? You did? Then you deserve a gold star, because it's the hardest one of all!

30. CLIPPED POINTS

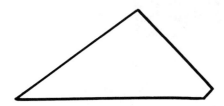 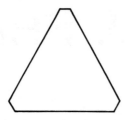  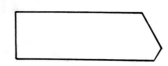

Many pattern pieces have the points clipped off. This saves a lot of guesswork because it creates two precisely-matched corners to sew together. If your seams are a consistent scant 1/4″, your finished angles will delight you—they will be perfect!

To rotary-cut these clipped-off points, just tape you template along any straight edge.

This step is worth it!

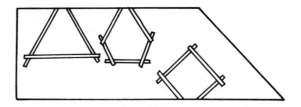

DONNA'S SCRAP QUILT SOUP

Whenever I see a few days coming that I can grab for a quilting orgy, I DO it! During that time there is no housework, no cleaning, no laundry, and NO cooking!

To keep my family from feeling neglected I make, the day before, a gigantic pot of soup. There's something very warm and homey about dipping into this "farmhouse" meal—it kind of goes with quilting.

I'm not an enthusiastic cook, but I do enjoy making soup. The rave reviews I get help, of course!

So—for all of my quilting buddies—here's:

DONNA'S SCRAP QUILT SOUP

A few notes:

1. I chop EVERYTHING but the meat into 1/2″ to 1″ pieces. Don't be fussy, just get it chopped up.

2. I use ALL of the scallions and celery. The tops and leaves of these two are the BEST seasonings.

3. The amounts and selections I've given are my personal favorites. Vary these to please your family's tastes.

4. No two pots of my soups are alike. It all depends on what veggies are in season.

5. This is a good time to clean out the refrigerator. "Old" veggies do just fine in soups.

6. There are two "secrets" to my soup. One: except for a can of crushed tomatoes, I try to use only fresh veggies in my soup—even the corn! Two: the veggies, themselves, are used as the thickening agent, adding marvelous flavor with every bite.

OK, here we go: In a 10-quart pot, I put:
- 6 QUARTS WATER
- 3 BUNCHES SCALLIONS (1 pound)
- 1 LARGE BUNCH CELERY
- 6 BOULLION CUBES, if desired, for seasoning (I add chicken cubes if I use chicken and beef cubes if I use beef)
- 1 LARGE CAN CRUSHED TOMATOES (optional)

Bring this to boiling, then continue on "simmer." This is the base of every pot of soup I make, no matter what kind it will become.

Next, add some sort of meat. I go fairly light on

this—1 to 2 pounds. (Trim the fat off of the beef and the skin off of the chicken.) If I'm using beef, I like to brown it in a separate pan before adding it to the soup. Leave the meat in large chunks because you'll want to remove it later. I choose from:

- CHICKEN (my favorites are thighs or breasts)
- HAM
- BEEF (almost any kind of pot roast)

Next, add veggies until the pot is as full as you'd like it, adding water as needed. You can use any veggies, but my favorites are:

- TOMATOES (1 to 2 lbs.)
- STRING BEANS (1 to 1-1/2 lbs.)
- CARROTS (1 to 1-1/2 lbs.)
- CORN (kernels from 4 to 6 cobs)
- LIMA BEANS (1 to 1-1/2 lbs.)
- POTATOES (1 to 1-1/2 lbs.)
- BROCCOLI (1 to 1-1/2 lbs.)
- CAULIFLOWER (1/2 to 1 lb.)
- SUMMER SQUASH (3 to 4)
- SPLIT PEAS (2 pounds—these must be soaked 1 hour first)

Next, add seasonings to taste.
- SALT (I use this as lightly as possible)
- BLACK PEPPER (This is one of our favorite seasonings, so I use quite a bit)

Simmer all of this 2 to 3 hours. Sometime during the last half of the cooking time:

1. Remove meat, cut into small pieces, set aside.
2. Remove half of veggies, puree, and put back in soup with meat.
3. Add a grain or pasta. I like these best:
- RICE (medium or long grain)
- BARLEY
- NOODLES (any kind)

Here are some of my favorite combinations (don't forget the scallions and celery!)

1. Ham, split peas, carrots, potatoes
2. Beef, tomatoes, string beans, carrots, corn, barley
3. Chicken, corn, tomatoes, rice.

Now—leave this with a loaf or two of Italian bread and a bowl of fresh fruit. Your family will love it! And you can go off and SEW!

GLOSSARY

Backing: The fabric used on the underside of the quilt.

Baste: Temporarily secure three layers together so they can be handled while quilting, often done with long stitching.

Batting: The layer between the quilt top and the backing. Gives the quilt its "puffiness."

Bias: Diagonal to the grain.

Binding: Enclosing the fabric and batting of the outer border to create a finished edge.

Block: A quilt square made of a number of smaller pieces sewn together.

Borders: Fabric used around outer areas of quilt to highlight central area and to enlarge the quilt to desired size.

Grain: The direction of either the horizontal or vertical threads of the fabric. Will be either parallel to the selvage or at a 90° angle to it.

Lattice: Narrow strips sewn between blocks, used to add color and to highlight the blocks.

Lattice blocks: Small squares connecting the lattice strips.

Layout: The arrangement of blocks, units, lattice, and borders that make up the quilt top.

Piecing: Stitching the small pieces of fabric together.

Pin-baste: Basting with safety pins. Holds more securely than thread basting. Machine foot will not catch in the basting thread.

Quilt center: The pieced quilt, before any borders are added.

Quilting: Stitching the three layers—quilt top, batting, and backing—together.

Selvage: The woven edge along the length of the fabric.

Stitch-in-the-ditch: Quilting done in a seamline.

Template: The pattern for each piece in a block or quilt.

SUPPLY LIST

SPEED-CUTTING EQUIPMENT

Please check your local quilt store for the Miterite and templates. If not in stock, they are available through:

Holiday Designs
Rt. 1, Box 302P
Mineola, TX 75773

Check quilting and sewing magazines for current mail-order companies. Here are some good ones for general quilting supplies:

Clotilde
1-800-772-2891
1-800-863-3191 (fax)

Crafts Americana
13118 NE 4th St.
Vancouver, WA 98684
(360) 260-8900

Keepsake Quilting
Rt. 25, Box 1618
Centre Harbor, NH 03226
(603) 253-4026

Treadle Art
25834 Narbonne Ave.
Lomita, CA 90717
(310) 534-5122

BIBLIOGRAPHY

Fanning, Robbie and Tony. *The Complete Book of Machine Quilting*. Radnor, PA: Chilton Book Co., 1980.

Hargrave, Harriet. *Heirloom Machine Quilting*. Martinez, CA: C&T Publishing, 1990.

Hopkins, Mary Ellen. *The It's Okay If You Sit on My Quilt Book*. Cardiff by the Sea, CA: ME Publications, 1989.

Johannah, Barbara. *Barbara Johannah's Crystal Piecing*. Radnor, PA: Chilton Book Co., 1993.

Johnson-Srebro, Nancy. *Rotary Magic*. Emmaus, PA: Rodale Press, Inc., 1998.

McClun, Diana and Laura Nownes. *Quilts!Quilts!!Quilts!!!* Lincolnwood, IL: Quilt Digest Press, 1988.

Michell, Marti. *Quilting for People Who Don't Have Time To Quilt*. San Marcos, CA: American School of Needlework, 1988.

Poster, Donna. *Stars Galore and Even More*. Radnor, PA: Chilton Book Co., 1995.

Seward, Linda. *Patchwork, Quilting and Appliqué*. New York: Prentice-Hall, 1987.

Tyrrell, Judy. *Beginner's Guide to Machine Quilting*. San Marcos, CA: American School of Needlework, 1990.